Taking Chances

The Psychology of Losing and How to Profit from It

Dr. Robert T. Lewis

Houghton Mifflin Company Boston   1979

Library of Congress Cataloging in Publication Data
Lewis, Robert T
  Taking chances.
  Includes bibliographical references and index.
  1. Failure (Psychology) I. Title.
BF575.F14L48   158′.1   78-32066
ISBN 0-395-27606-3

Printed in the United States of America

V 10 9 8 7 6 5 4 3 2 1

Preface

Throughout history, acclaim and honor have been bestowed upon the man or woman who, through strength, courage, cunning, or intelligence, managed to conquer lesser competitors. In ancient times, the battle cry was, "To the victor go the spoils!" Today, the overemphasis on victory is epitomized by the quotation attributed to the late Vince Lombardi, former coach of the Green Bay Packers, "Winning isn't everything. It's the *only* thing."

In any contest there are at least as many losers as winners, often more. Yet the media inevitably give a disproportionate amount of coverage to the winner. Losers are all but forgotten. Information on how to win outweighs data on how and why we lose by a wide margin. To help offset that imbalance, I decided to write this book.

While books on winning are read voraciously by people who see themselves as losers and think life would be much better if they only learned how to win, this volume is designed for winners and losers alike since we can learn by either winning or losing. It is an attempt to explore the psychological reasons why we set ourselves up to lose when we think we are trying to win, and it shows how we can profit from losing. Its underlying philosophy is that we should strive to win but not feel humiliated when we lose. To win is admirable, but by losing occasionally we become more human. Therefore, be thankful nobody's perfect.

Dr. Robert T. Lewis

Newport Beach, California

Contents

PART I

The Psychology
of Losing

We have forty million reasons for failure,
but not a single excuse.
— *Rudyard Kipling*

Chapter 1

Win Some, Lose Some

For most Americans, *lose* is a four-letter word! No one but masochists and weight watchers enjoy it. Yet everyone does it.

America is a success-oriented culture. It places great value on being the fastest, the first, the biggest, the best. It extols the triumphs over adversity of Horatio Alger and Abraham Lincoln. In such a highly competitive society, there is a stigma placed on losing.

Everyone loses sometimes, of course. After all, to err is human. We get passed over for promotion, drop a little money in a poker game, or lock our keys in our car. But most of us try to hide our mistakes and failings since those who are known to lose frequently are often shunned, much as if they had a social disease. For instance, when the Worden, Illinois, high-school basketball team had a particularly bad year, they not only lost all twenty-one games they played, but to add humiliation to defeat, even the school cheerleaders quit and refused to attend the games.[1] After all, who wants to be identified with a loser?

Yet for every winner there must be a loser. Usually, more than one. And, while the winner is basking in the sweet glow of victory, the losers generally sink slowly into oblivion. For every Romeo who gains immortality for having lost both his life and his Juliet, there are thousands of losers who go unsung. Only rarely is a loser like mighty Casey, who lost the crucial game for Mudville by striking out with the bases loaded in the ninth inning, remembered while the pitcher who accomplished that momentous feat is forgotten.

While most of us prefer not to admit it, we lose more often than we win. The only ones who never fail are the ones who never compete. Or as the late humorist and playwright George Ade once said, "Anyone can win, unless there happens to be a second entry." Like winning, losing is a human condition. However, since losing is so unpopular, we tend to ignore it and pretend it can't happen. Unless, of course, it happens to someone else.

People lose for many reasons. Sometimes they are overmatched and find themselves competing with opponents who have superior ability or more experience. Sometimes losing is due to an error in judgment, such as the driver of a Volkswagen in Los Angeles made when he tried to maneuver between two cars parked at a stop light. Although scraped fenders are not uncommon on busy Los Angeles streets, this particular driver managed to hit not only the Cadillac on his right, but also the Cadillac on his left. Some people fail because they lack sufficient evidence upon which to make the correct decision. Still others seem to have an unconscious need to fail and to be punished. Yet in spite of the prevalence of losing behavior and the many reasons for it, there is little factual research or information available on the subject.

In recent years formerly tabooed subjects and behavior like homosexuality and death and dying have come out of the closet and have achieved a certain amount of respectability. It is slowly becoming acceptable to express aggressive feelings in certain situations, recognizing that bottling them up and striving too hard to become a "nice guy" can cause a person considerable physical and psychological damage. Even personal hangups about money have received some attention. Many types of human behavior that were formerly discussed objectively only in the college classroom, if at all, are now dealt with candidly in everyday conversation. But who talks about losing — except in a derogatory manner?

Win, Win, Win

The sacred cow of winning at all costs has taken a heavy toll on society. Many capable people drop out of society because they feel they cannot live up to the unrealistic expectations they set for themselves or others set for them. Some resort to a life of fantasy because they feel like failures in reality. It is estimated that one out of every ten Americans has emotional problems severe enough to warrant professional help. One out of every eight adults is on the way to becoming an alcoholic. Large numbers of adolescents, who are insecure and who feel inadequate, turn to drugs and alcohol to help them cope with a world they don't feel they can manage on their own. Suicide is the third leading cause of death among college-age individuals. These young people see themselves as failures and give up on themselves and life before they have really lived.

The win-at-all-costs philosophy places a heavy strain on morality. When winning becomes too important, the temptation to cheat increases. If the end justifies the means, deception and dishonesty can be rationalized away. Regulations and controls then become necessary to enforce fair competition. Athletes and horses are required to take urinalysis tests to discourage an unfair advantage from the use of certain drugs. In high-level contract bridge tournaments, the players are separated by a screen so they cannot give hand signals and a barrier is placed along the bottom of the table so they cannot give signals by kicking each other. In a recent bridge tournament players were found giving illicit information by means of a series of sniffs and coughs.[2] Too often the competition among players becomes secondary to that between players and officials. Players who attempt to break or circumvent the rules of the game "win" if their deceptions go undetected and "lose" if they get caught.

Perhaps as important as the threat to moral standards is the fact that overemphasis on winning takes much of the fun out of competing. It is not uncommon for parents of opposing teams at a Little League baseball game to be at each other's throats and to scream for their offspring to commit mayhem on their rivals. Fortunately, at this age, children usually have a better perspective on the game than do their parents. While the adults are glowing with victory or glowering in defeat, the players are likely to walk off the field arm in arm with members of their own and the other team, discussing important issues like where to go swimming or what flavor ice cream to buy. To them, a game is a game is a game.

Little League baseball, Pop Warner football, and similar organizations were formed to encourage greater participation in athletics, teach fundamentals, build character, teach sportsmanship, and achieve other noble results. Too often, however, these goals have been sacrificed because of the obsession to win on the part of parents and coaches. Under adult guidance, spontaneity gives way to regimentation. The enjoyment of playing becomes secondary to winning.

When Tommy was eight, he enjoyed playing catch with his father. He also enjoyed swimming, raising frogs, playing spaceman, and numerous other activities. However, when his father promised him a new baseball glove and a chance to wear a uniform, Tommy agreed to give up some of his other activities and join a Little League baseball team. He disliked it intensely when the coach yelled at him for dropping the ball or for striking out, but to please his father he kept trying and didn't quit the team. Although it was the stated policy that everyone who practiced would be allowed to play, Tommy and some of the other players were overlooked. They sat on the bench, bored and hot, while the better athletes were competing on the field. Tommy was embarrassed when he heard his father bragging about how "My son's team is winning the pennant!" And he didn't know what to think when he heard his coach tell a parent, "The younger and more inexperienced kids would rather sit on the bench and watch their team win than play themselves and risk losing." Tommy felt very confused since he *knew* that he and his friends would rather have the fun of playing.

After being exposed to the adult attitude about winning over a number of years, however, Tommy gradually learned to play for blood rather than for fun.

The obsession with success and winning cuts across all human dimensions — age, occupation, sex, and socioeconomic levels. Parents compete with each other to see who is the baby's favorite and with other parents to see whose baby is toilet trained first. Schoolchildren vie with each other to see who gets the highest grades, runs the fastest, is the most popular, or the best looking. For many politicians, winning elections is more important than is the process of governing. Some spend more money to become elected than they make in their term of office. Cities strive to become the biggest in the country or in the world, even though financial and social problems increase out of proportion to the increase in population. Businesses do the same. Winning can be interpreted as having the best job, the most money, the biggest house, the most expensive car, or living on the right side of town. Whatever a person has or does, it is likely to be best by some standard. Few of us admit that we might be average or mediocre in anything, and certainly not inferior.

The overemphasis on winning causes many individuals to avoid competing. Rather than risk the humiliation of defeat, they sit on the sidelines of life and exclude themselves from activities they might otherwise enjoy. And, in some cases, the cost is more than just the lack of pleasure. Dr. Ralph A. Nelson, Associate Professor of Nutrition at the Mayo Medical School, conducted a five-year study of obese children. He concluded that many of these children failed to develop proper habits of exercise because they became discouraged in trying to compete with superior athletes. They then lost interest in physical education and physical fitness and were unable to burn off excess calories.[3]

Success in the adult world is frequently judged by one's finances. The more money people have, the more important they are likely to appear to be in the eyes of others. How the money was acquired is of secondary importance. It makes little difference whether it was earned honestly or dishonestly or not earned at all. Since one's net worth is the most widely accepted measure of success, the John D. Rockefellers of the world are generally thought to outshine the John Does.

But what is the price of success by such standards? For those who desire power and riches but who are not fortunate enough to inherit them, winning too often leads to dehumanization. People who are determined to overcome all obstacles en route to success are forced to devote an excessive amount of time and energy to the task. To stay ahead, one often must repress emotions, curb extracurricular interests, and forego intimate relationships.

With the tremendous competition for the few spots at the

top, single-minded determination to reach the peak is a necessity. All other considerations and values must, in most cases, be seen merely as deterrents that are likely to prevent one from reaching the goal. Tenderness, humility, warmth, and compassion are seen either as signs of weakness or as luxuries the person obsessed with winning cannot afford.

For those who see themselves as failures but who are determined to become winners, there is a lot of help available. Books on winning, becoming successful, and making fortunes fill the shelves of bookstores and newsstands. Thousands of teachers, coaches, executives, and consultants devote their lives to making losers into winners of one sort or another. Millions of dollars are spent each year on psychotherapy by people who feel inadequate because they have not achieved some fantastic goal. Formulas for success and systems for winning abound. Even for animals who have a thing about winning, help is available. A "horse psychiatrist" who turned a thoroughbred, a recent loser by forty-one lengths, into a winner worth $200,000 claims:

> When a horse wins, you can really tell he's happy. He raises his eyebrows, he sleeps peacefully in the afternoon. You can tell he doesn't have mental worries.
>
> By losing, a horse can build up negative anxiety or tension. It scares hell out of him and he builds up a fear and tries to get the hell off the track. You have to turn it into positive anxiety.[4]

But little help has been available for people who lose and want to profit from the experience.

Losing as a Growth Experience

Losing, like winning, is a part of living. As such, it should provide an opportunity to learn about oneself and one's capabilities. In most cases, there is nothing inherently good or bad about either winning or losing. The judgment is most often solely in the mind of the perceiver. What looks like success to one person may appear to be failure to another. A story that has been around for many years and has been told with many variations illustrates the point. A recent version involves two men, an American and a Russian, who were to run a race. When the race was run, the American won. Following the victory, an American newspaper ran the headline, AMERICAN WINS; RUSSIAN FINISHES LAST, while a Russian headline announced, RUSSIAN PLACES SECOND; AMERICAN IS NEXT TO LAST.

Of even more importance than whether you actually win or lose is the *value* you attribute to it. Ideally, if you fail to achieve an objective, you should assess your loss realistically. Instead of blaming others or shouting, "I was robbed!" or "I have the damnedest luck!" you should say something like "I'm really unhappy I lost. I wanted to win and I tried hard to do so. Is it worth it to try again, or should I forget it and try something else? If I try again, what can I learn from my failure? How can I improve my performance?"

Too often, however, when we feel we have lost, we are so shattered by the experience that we also lose our perspective. We are no longer objective or rational about either ourselves or our losses. In the vernacular of Albert Ellis, founder of Rational-Emotive Therapy, we follow our objective statement, "I lost, and I'm sorry I lost," with an irrational statement, such as "Therefore, I am a terrible, awful person — a nogoodnick!"[5] This kind of self-devaluation prevents us from making a realistic appraisal of our performance and it becomes impossible to learn or grow from it. On the other hand, by exploring the dynamics of losing and its positive as well as negative potential, it is often possible to change our perceptions so that most failures can be viewed as growth experiences.

Benefits of Overcoming the Fear of Losing

The fear of failure is a major deterrent to living life to its fullest. The stigma placed on losing and the obsession with winning pervade every aspect of life. In the words of the nineteenth-century American statesman Charles Francis Adams, "Failure seems to be regarded as the one unpardonable crime, success as the all redeeming virtue." By putting winning and losing in their proper perspective, the following are some of the possible benefits:

1. We can grow and learn from losing as well as from winning. Not only is learning often motivated by a desire to overcome failure and frustration, but by analyzing why we failed in a particular situation it is possible to correct our errors and avoid repeating them in the future.

2. Losing to an opponent of superior ability can be more rewarding than winning over a rival who has less talent or skill. Matching ourselves against a superior opponent provides us with the challenge to perform at top level rather than with complacency. It pushes us to improve our game and to learn additional skills.

3. We can enjoy competition for itself. The stimulation of exercise and challenge, either physical, mental, or both, can be rewarding regardless of whether we win or lose.

4. By reducing the fear of losing we actually increase our chances of winning. Since life is a gamble, it is necessary to risk losing in order to have the chance to win.

5. Losing occasionally is likely to enhance the joy of winning. If we won all the time, winning would be taken for granted and the thrill and excitement would soon diminish. The contrast between defeat and victory makes the "high" of winning higher.

6. Losing part of the time makes us more human. It ensures a feeling of humility. It makes us aware of our limitations and demonstrates how we are dependent upon others for what we lack ourselves. Our humility and compassion make others around us feel needed, and relationships with others will be enriched.

Chapter 2

Who's Number One?

Losing and winning are usually thought of as opposite positions on some kind of a scale. Although it is possible to talk about a man "losing his mind" or a person who "got lost" while trying to find an address in a strange town, losing and winning generally refer to the outcome of some competitive struggle.

Competition is such an integral part of American life that most of us are unaware of the extent to which we are caught up in it. We struggle to see who can stay in bed the longest in the morning, fight to be first in the bathroom, rush to gulp down breakfast the fastest. We push to get ahead of others on the subway or outmaneuver other cars on the freeway. We vie with competitors for the biggest share of the market in whatever field of endeavor we make our livelihood, or compete with fellow employees for promotions and raises. When not trying to outdo our neighbors with the biggest television set or the biggest roses, we compete with ourselves to up our sales quota or lower our golf scores.

The origins of competitive behavior are not fully understood. Aggression is obviously involved, but it also is not fully understood. Although social scientists have been debating whether aggression is learned or inherited, the bulk of the evidence suggests that the *capacity* for aggression is something we are born with. How, when, and to what degree it is expressed is learned. A group of psychologists at Yale University, led by Dr. John Dollard, concluded that aggression always occurs when we are frustrated.[1] Known as the *frustration-aggression hypothesis,* this theory maintains that some form of aggression is initiated whenever we are unable to achieve some goal or complete some task that we set out to accomplish. While aggression is linked with attack and anger, the aggressive behavior is not always conscious or overt.

In the 1920s, the physiologist W. B. Cannon discovered that hormonal changes take place in the body when we feel threatened or under stress. These changes prepare us to either attack or withdraw in the face of danger.[2] They are the result of adrenalin and noradrenalin from the adrenal gland being secreted into the bloodstream and are accompanied by emotions of fear, anger, or a combination of the two. Some endocrinologists suspect that adrenalin is related to fear and noradrenalin to anger, and that the emotional response a person has to a given stress situation depends on the proportional amount of each hormone in the system.[3] Whether the excess of adrenalin or noradrenalin is inherent or triggered by previous learning is still not known.

It has been found that rabbits, who tend to flee when threatened, have a higher proportion of adrenalin than noradrenalin in their systems. Lions, who are more likely to stand and fight, have an imbalance favoring noradrenalin. While this evidence lends itself to some interesting speculation, it has not been established conclusively that people who are meek, timid, and fearful, and hence more prone to lose than their more aggressive counterparts, have nervous systems genetically programmed to produce more adrenalin and less noradrenalin in the face of stress.

To survive in ancient times, a certain amount of aggression was necessary for humans, as it still is with lower animals. Living as we do in the nuclear age, our aggressive instincts must be directed into constructive growth and change or we may someday destroy ourselves. One of the areas often cited as a suitable outlet for sublimated aggression is athletic competition. Millions of people throughout the world engage in some type of competitive sport — either directly or vicariously. The aim is still to win over one's "enemy," but winning is no longer a matter of life or death — although players and spectators sometimes lose sight of that fact.

In the jungle the loser often winds up as dinner for the victor. Today, this is rarely true of humans, although Gordon Brown, a rugby player in Troon, Scotland, came close to being the exception. A week or so following a particularly rugged rugby match, Brown's leg began to fester and swell. Upon investigation, a local surgeon found the cause to be an opponent's tooth, root and all, embedded in Brown's limb.[4]

Why Be Number One?

People compete for all sorts of prizes — blue ribbons, loving cups, money, power, or fame — as well as for survival. The earliest and most important reward for winning in the lives of most people, however, and the one that sets the tone for all other competitive struggles, is parental approval and affection. The need for approval from parents and others upon whom a child is dependent is an outgrowth of a basic survival instinct. Those infants who are looked on most favorably by their parents and their environment are most likely to survive. The odds are reduced for those who are ignored or rejected. Besides needing protection from physical danger, infants who have not had adequate body contact and mothering may develop marasmus, a disorder characterized by apathy and a loss of interest in food and surroundings. Children who develop this condition seem to lose the will to live, and some even die.

Competition for parental approval is the basis of sibling rivalry, although the rivalry may take many forms and center around issues that tend to obscure the underlying goal. Competition to be the best student or the best athlete or the child who is best adjusted socially stems from the assumption that whoever wins will be favored by one or both parents.

In addition to its direct relevance to intrafamily struggles, the need for parental approval and affection gradually dissipates, merges into, and indirectly affects a myriad of other emotional and psychological needs and desires, such as security, self-esteem, power, love, pride, and social approval. The degree of frustration or satisfaction incurred in seeking parental approval will help determine the intensity of our subsequent needs and the extent to which we will compete for their satisfaction. Other things being equal, *the overly competitive individual is one who received some, but not enough, parental approval in early childhood, and who had to earn what was received through some form of achievement.* Children who receive an abundance of approval with no effort have no reason to demand or struggle to get more. Those who *never* win approval are inclined to give up and quit trying.

Not infrequently, the highly successful, highly competitive skater, swimmer, or tennis player is pushed to stardom by a demanding, overly zealous parent who is quick to criticize but gives praise sparingly and grudgingly. Such parents are not content that their children win in whatever competition they enter but are only satisfied with perfection. They focus on the child's faults and shortcomings rather than successes. No matter how hard they try or how well they play, these children rarely have the feeling of having pleased their parents. It is from this background that the "winning is the only thing" attitude evolves. By internalizing parental values, the children also learn to judge anything less than perfect on their part as unacceptable.

Learning Through Failure

Contrary to what one might think, a certain amount of failure is necessary for psychological growth. While it is true that too much failure will overwhelm and demoralize a person, too much success, on the other hand, tends to make an individual complacent and resistant to change. Why change a winning system? What would be the motivation?

We change and grow because we are dissatisfied with the way things are or with the way we feel about some aspect of our lives. Under normal conditions, we are inclined to continue doing the things that are rewarding to us, to perpetuate the kinds of experiences we deem successful. By contrast, we try to change the things that are frustrating and unpleasant and that fail to provide us with a feeling of satisfaction. The ability to change and to progress is an integral part of growing. It involves the capacity to profit from our mistakes and to overcome obstacles and failures. Without failure and frustration, we would stagnate. Or, as the eminent essayist and journalist the late Christopher Morley put it, "High heels were invented by a woman who had been kissed on the forehead."

The infant makes his or her needs known primarily by crying. If, however, in progressing from infancy to childhood, and ultimately into adulthood, all needs could still be satisfied by crying, other methods of satisfaction might never be learned. Instead of going to the store, buying food, and cooking it, the person would simply cry. However, even the most permissive parents sooner or later communicate to their children that crying is not the magic wand that makes all desires and dreams come true. It is because crying *fails* to bring the desired results that children are forced to learn more socially approved behavior in order to satisfy their desires and overcome their frustrations.

One of the primary differences between adults and infants is the wider range of behavior the adult has learned in order to cope with the problems and demands of living. Many philosophers contend that learning and growing are the essence of living. And psychologists have learned that a particular behavior is learned because in some way it is rewarding, while alternative behaviors are either less rewarding or not rewarding at all. The *motive* for learning, however, is most often the anxiety or discomfort caused by frustration, conflict, or failure. The reward is the reduction or elimination of these negative feelings. When the prevailing behavior fails to provide pleasure or satisfaction, a state of tension develops. It is this state of tension that motivates people to learn other types of behavior that will prove rewarding. Therefore, without some loss and failure, learning is unlikely to take place.

When failures seem so overwhelming that they cannot be overcome with the normal amount of effort and motivation, we may become depressed and feel that there is nothing we can do to alter the events in our lives in a more favorable way. We are likely to conclude that our failure is due to a lack of ability rather than a lack of effort on our part. In attempting to help people overcome this negative attitude, a failure-free retraining program has been devised. The rationale for the program is that a constant exposure to success would overcome a person's ingrained feeling of helplessness and failure. A recent study, however, found that children with "learned helplessness" responded better when some failure was intermingled with success. The conclusion was that errorless learning was probably shortsighted. The inclusion of failure allows children to deal with life realistically and to develop a feeling that with increased effort they can overcome failure.[5]

Where It Doesn't Pay to Win

The importance attributed to winning depends to a large extent upon the culture to which one belongs. A competitive attitude and an obsessive desire to win are learned. While the desire for parental approval and acceptance motivates children to behave competitively, this only holds true where parents, in tune with cultural mores, place great value on being first or best. In cultures that emphasize the importance of the individual rather than the group or the society, differences, rather than similarities, among people are stressed. This, in turn, encourages comparisons and value judgments as to which differences are better. In cultures that encourage everyone to be alike, such comparisons are impossible.

To anyone familiar only with the American way of life, with its roots in the sanctity of individual rights and responsibilities and its competitive, achievement-oriented value system, the idea of a culture where winning is taboo might seem strange indeed. Yet a number of such cultures exist.

The Hutterites, a close-knit religious sect that migrated from Russia to the Dakotas, Montana, and Canada, deemphasize individual attainment. All property is community owned and initiative and competition are discouraged. In mainland China, pressure on children to conform to the group norm is applied by the family, the school, and the state. Society is placed before the individual, and individual differences are minimized. Among the Wintun Indians of northern California, there is little distinction between the self and the nonself. The person merges with the environment and the world rather than being distinct from it. And the Wintun language makes limited use of the words *I* and *my*.

The Dakota Indians, particularly before being confined to a reservation, maintained a culture based on beliefs and values very similar to those held by Eastern mystics. They perceived themselves as being related to all things. They thought in terms of a oneness with the universe and submerged their individuality. Individual achievement was not recognized, and there was no reward for being first or best or strongest in a competitive sense. When the United States Government introduced formal education to the Dakota tribes, white teachers were dumbfounded by the Indian children's attitudes. If children were sent to the blackboard to work arithmetic problems and told to turn around when they were finished, the children would wait until everyone was finished and all would turn around together. If encouraged to run a race, the fastest child would hesitate near the finish line until the others caught up. Winning more than once at anything would cause the child to lose face.

This is a far cry from the attitude of the Marine Corps officer who fired off an angry letter to a sportswriter for a large metropolitan newspaper. He called the writer "a dirty communist" for printing a column critical of the overemphasis on winning in today's society.

While a group-oriented culture fits the needs of some societies and some people, every culture has its drawbacks as well as its advantages. What is gained in group security in cultures that foster it is lost in individual freedom and the opportunity to maximize one's potential. While the emphasis on winning has been exaggerated in America and most of the Western world, competition is an integral part of our culture. A more realistic attitude toward winning and losing rather than the elimination of competition would seem to be the most reasonable goal for most of us in our society.

When in Rome . . .

Not only does the culture dictate acceptable and unacceptable limits of competition and aggression, it also defines what is considered winning and losing behavior. In the United States, bigamy is a criminal offense, and a man who has more than one wife is a likely candidate for jail. Among the Zulus, however, polygamy is sanctioned, and the man who can afford only one wife is considered a loser. Americans generally associate steak with success and affluence, while the Ifugao of Luzon would probably choose crickets, beetles, or red ants for a victory celebration. The genius, by urban American standards, might not have the kind of intelligence needed to survive two days in the jungles of Brazil. Likewise, the big winner from the jungle would most likely be a loser in New York City.

Along with luck and money, intelligence is generally considered one of the major keys to success. In modern society those possessing sufficient intelligence have been encouraged to obtain an ever increasing amount of formal education in order to cope better with a complex and demanding world. For years a college education has been considered the Great White Way to success and riches. Thousands of young people have been coerced and bribed into entering the halls of higher learning against their natural predilection. Those whose intelligence or academic preparation was inadequate to gain admission, or to maintain a minimum grade-point average after having been admitted, were seen as failures and relegated to the role of second-class citizens.

In many parts of the world, education is still seen as a privilege rather than a right or an obligation. Children fortunate enough to receive a higher education in underdeveloped countries are being prepared for positions of leadership. In many cultures competitive examinations, taken at an early age, determine the future course of a child's life: whether the person will progress to higher education, be sent to a trade school, or be destined to perform common labor.

In America, as is generally true in other fast-moving, industrialized countries, intelligence is considered to be highly correlated with verbal fluency. Intelligence tests are heavily weighted with academically oriented items, which demand achievement in the classical three Rs in order to be answered correctly. Vocabulary usage is found to be the best single predictor of general intelligence in this country. Recent understanding of how the human brain functions, however, indicates that most formal education and most of what is considered intelligence applies only to half of the brain.

The brain consists of two hemispheres connected by a large bundle of fibers. The left hemisphere controls the functions of the right side of the body. In addition, in the vast majority of individuals (some left-handed persons are exceptions), the left hemisphere is "predominantly involved with analytic, logical thinking, especially in verbal and mathematical functions." [6]

The other side of the brain, the right hemisphere, has largely been ignored in educational and intellectual circles. Those whose abilities are related to the right rather than the left hemisphere have too often been considered not intelligent and inferior. Until recently the functions of the right hemisphere have been less well understood. The right hemisphere processes information more diffusely than does the left hemisphere and is primarily responsible for performing visuo-spatial tasks. A strong right hemisphere is essential for artistic and creative endeavors, orientation in space, and for perceiving relationships and patterns as wholes rather than as parts.

Although both hemispheres work together to a large degree, most of us show a decided preference for using one or the other in problem-solving situations. Western cultures are primarily left-brain-oriented, while Eastern cultures, which are more reflective and mystical, tend to favor the right brain. Therefore, whether you are considered a winner or a loser depends partly on having the hemisphere preference that is lauded by the culture or subculture in which you live, although it is not known if such preferences are genetically determined or learned. In addition, the person who aspires to become a jazz musician, a belly dancer, a second Rembrandt, a star quarterback, a Zen master, or a forest ranger would do well to have a highly developed right hemisphere, while the prospective attorney, bookkeeper, engineer, or schoolteacher requires a well-developed left hemisphere to avoid becoming a loser.

Winning and losing are rarely simple processes. Some people lose more than others, and winning sometimes depends on being in the right place at the right time. In most cases, however, both winning and losing behaviors are the end result of many complex and interrelated factors. In addition to determination, motivation, and other psychological variables, the time and culture in which one lives play a significant role in determining whether a particular behavior warrants the accolade of success, the derision of failure, or enjoyment merely as a noncompetitive experience.

Chapter 3

Losing Is in the
Eye of the Beholder

Like beauty, success or failure is in the eye of the beholder. What is a victory for one may seem like defeat to another and vice versa. A high-school athlete who runs a mile in four and a half minutes might well consider it a great accomplishment, but a world-class distance runner would view the same time as a very poor showing. Judged by his teachers in school, Albert Einstein was a failure. Judged by the world for his later accomplishments, he was acclaimed a genius. In business circles, an executive who commands a large salary will most likely be perceived as a success. During a divorce proceeding, however, the spouse may claim the person is a failure as a provider, lover, and responsible family member.

Despite instant replays and sophisticated electronic measuring and timing devices, decisions on winning and losing performances are not always based on objective evidence. Whether viewing the behavior of another or looking at oneself in the mirror, the evaluation is largely subjective. The real winners are not always the ones who wind up with the most chips or the most blue ribbons. For example, the Bible raises the question, "What is a man profited, if he shall gain the whole world, and lose his own soul?" [1] In the final analysis, victory or defeat, winning or losing, is, in the parlance of athletics, a judgment call. In many cases the person making that call is not the umpire or the referee, but the person who performed the deed, wrote the book, or ran the race.

In judging our own performance, it is not uncommon to use a much more demanding criterion than we use to measure the accomplishments of others. We are frequently more tolerant of the mistakes, errors, and shortcomings of other people than we are of our own. Regardless of how the world views our performance, if it is less than our own expectations, realistic or otherwise, we are inclined to perceive ourselves as failures. Franz Kafka, the famous German-Czech novelist, thought so little of his literary efforts that he urged they all be burned after his death. Claude Monet, the leading French Impressionist, whose paintings sell today for hundreds of thousands of dollars, believed his life to have been nothing but a failure. Even Leonardo da Vinci, whose genius spanned almost all the arts and sciences, claimed, "I have offended God and mankind because my work didn't reach the quality it should have."

Insuring Failure

People who consistently fall short of their goals often set themselves up to fail by aspiring to achieve unrealistic levels of success. Too often the goal is perfection. The student who is dissatisfied with anything less than a perfect score in every exam, the salesperson who expects to make a sale to every prospect, and the golfer who is determined to win every tournament are all likely to spend more time being frustrated and feeling defeated than being satisfied with their achievements. People who expect perfection of themselves make it all but impossible to win. A grade of ninety-five on a calculus test may rate an A from the teacher, but to the student who demands perfection it is less than perfect and therefore a failure.

Ronald was a junior in one of the nation's top technical and scientific institutions, majoring in nuclear physics. One afternoon he was found running across the campus, rambling incoherently, and apparently oblivious to everything and everyone around him. When he was coerced into going to the infirmary and given medication to calm him down, Ronald began making suicidal threats.

Under the care of a psychiatrist, it became clear that Ronald's psychotic episode was triggered by his failure to correctly answer *one* physics problem. It seems that his whole identity was contingent upon his reputation as a "brain." He was awkward socially and physically, but his intellect was superior. In all his nineteen years he had never met a mathematical or science problem he could not master. Consequently, he was totally unprepared for failure in this area, and he was shattered when he experienced it for the first time. Anxiety overwhelmed him and he was unable to cope. He considered himself a failure, and suicide seemed the only answer to his feeling of intense shame.

Ronald, like many individuals who set impossible goals for themselves, suffered from a negative self-image. Despite his academic success and his reputation for brilliance, he did not think of himself as a worthwhile person. Consequently, he tried to make up for his perceived lack of self-worth by winning accolades from others through intellectual accomplishments. When he failed to live up to his unrealistic and perfectionistic goal, he had nothing to fall back on.

The eminent existential psychologist Carl Rogers maintains that one of the characteristics of most neurotic individuals is an unrealistically high level of aspiration and an equally unrealistically low self-concept. This is a self-defeating system. When the person is unable to achieve an unattainable goal, it is perceived as failure and the person's low self-concept is lowered further. To compensate for the lowered self-concept, the level of aspiration is raised correspondingly. The individual now believes it necessary to reach this higher level of success in order to feel adequate. This, in turn, further insures the probability of failing. (Rogers sees one of the primary goals of psychotherapy as helping people bring their level of aspiration and their self-concept closer together so the possibility of failing unnecessarily is lessened and the self-concept can be strengthened.)

The Care and Feeding of a Negative Self-Concept

A number of authorities in the field of human behavior consider the self to be the core of personality. The self is seen as the integrating, unifying force in the development of personality and the filter through which all experiences are evaluated by the person. Perhaps the two foremost proponents of this point of view are psychologists Arthur Combs and Donald Snygg.[2] According to these theorists, the self is an outgrowth of the infant's perception of his or her interaction with the world. If the infant feels loved and secure, his or her needs are generally taken care of, and there is relative freedom from tension, a positive self-concept evolves. If neglected, the infant feels unwanted, unworthy, and insecure, and develops a negative conception of self.

Once a positive or negative self-concept is crystallized, it is difficult to modify. Situations, ideas, and experiences that are inconsistent with one's self-concept are ignored or rejected. Those with a negative self-concept are pessimistic, discount their successes, and expect to fail in whatever they attempt. They tend to react to other people with fear, timidity, and withdrawal or with anger and aggression. In either case, their negative behavior is likely to produce the rejection they anticipate, which further reinforces their negative self-concept. If, in spite of their negative outlook and behavior, they achieve some success they cannot deny, their concept of self is not totally changed. It is, however, modified. Now they see themselves as total failures *except* in this one area.

Tom Jenkins worked his way through college and maintained a B-plus average. He married the homecoming queen, became president of his own corporation, lived in the best part of town, and belonged to the finest country club. His children were attractive and intelligent and were respectful and loving toward him. His employees thought highly of him. Yet Tom still thought poorly of himself. Although his negative self-concept goaded him to achieve and to prove that he was a worthwhile person, his successes never completely changed his self-image. His negative perception of himself also affected his perception of every other aspect of his life to some degree. He had nagging fears that his wife would find him unattractive and leave him for another man. Every business setback was seen as a personal failure. He was chronically depressed because he wasn't making more money, increasing his business, spending more time with his wife, being a better model for his children, or contributing more to society.

A person's self-concept is a highly subjective perception and may not correlate with any objective measure of value or worth. It takes many, many positive experiences to offset an early negative perception of one's self. These experiences must have sufficient impact on the person that they cannot be ignored. Then they can be incorporated into the self-concept and can modify it to some degree. Under ordinary

circumstances, however, a change from a completely negative to a predominantly positive self-concept may never happen. Professional help may be required.

"A Time to Weep, and a Time to Laugh"

The ancient Greek essayist and philosopher Plutarch ad-
vised, "Be ruled by time, the wisest counselor of all." Nowhere is this more applicable than in the evaluation of losing behavior. Not only is it true that many situations that
look like disasters at the time turn out to be positive later
on, but yesterday's tragedies are today's humorous parlor
stories. The difference between tragedy and comedy is often
a matter of a few months or years.

The driver of a Brink's armored truck was more cha-
grined than amused when halted by the San Clemente, California, police. They had received an urgent message from a
company executive in Los Angeles asking their help in spot-
ting the vehicle. The urgent message had nothing to do with
a holdup, kidnapping, or truck theft, but a notice to the
driver stating, "You forgot the money." [3] The humor may
come later in telling the story to friends.

Alan Brown, an interior designer from Spokane, Washington, was not laughing when he went to see his dentist.
He had won a free trip to Ohio to see the Washington
State–Ohio State football game but gave up the prize when
he remembered he had a dental appointment. When he
showed up for the appointment, however, a receptionist
calmly told Brown the dentist was out of town. "You see,"
she said, "he won this drawing and he's in Ohio for the
football game." [4] Maybe someday Brown will look back on
the incident and laugh.

A near tragedy, with a somewhat humorous aftermath,

occurred at a Honolulu building project. A crane operator picked up a portable toilet and was winging it skyward when there was a sudden outburst of angry epithets from inside. The crane operator set the toilet down gingerly. After several anxious moments a man stepped out and hurried away. Apparently the only injury was to his pride.[5]

The series of calamities that happened in one afternoon to Jennifer Marley would do justice to an old Mack Sennett comedy. Having received a telegram that her husband's favorite uncle was arriving from Philadelphia that evening, Jennifer frantically began cleaning the house. When she plugged in the vacuum cleaner, there was no sound but a lot of smoke. In desperation, she piled her three small children into the station wagon and dashed to the local appliance store to purchase a new vacuum. By the time she arrived home with her new purchase, time and patience were running out but still she didn't panic. That happened a few minutes later when she uncrated the new vacuum and watched helplessly as it crumbled into a number of unassembled pieces.

With great effort she pulled herself together and put dim bulbs in the lamps, hoping desperately that the dirt on the carpet would not show. She next turned her attention to the peanut butter and jelly sandwich lying face down on the newly scrubbed kitchen floor and the stream of feathers pouring out of the torn pillow that sailed over her head. When her three-year-old son, Bobby, popped in the back door covered with grease and dirt, she corralled him and headed for the bathroom. She made the mistake of taking her eyes off him while she started the bath water. That gave him time to slip out of the house and run naked down the street in pursuit of the new blouse she had planned to wear that evening — which was draped over the back of the family dog. By the time she had retrieved Bobby and what was left of the blouse, the tub was overflowing like a miniature waterfall and making a small lake of the bathroom.

At that point Jennifer collapsed and gave in to the flood of tears she had been fighting to hold back. At dinner, however, when she recounted her escapade, she could not help but join in the laughter of her husband and his uncle. She was clearly the main attraction of the evening, and, as he departed, Uncle George assured Jennifer that he could not remember having spent a more enjoyable evening.

The ability to laugh at oneself and one's foibles helps lessen the impact of adversity — even though it may take the passage of time to see the humor in a given situation. Time heals not only because it soothes the pain and humiliation of defeat, but because it allows you to view a situation from a more distant and detached point of view. As the humorist James Thurber defined it, "Humor is emotional chaos remembered in tranquility."

Laughter is therapeutic also because it is an effective means of reducing stress and tension. The essence of humor is its incompatibility with the seriousness of life. Much of humor is founded on the distortion of reality, a fantastic perception of what might realistically be seen as a very serious situation. It relies on absurdity, incongruity, the unexpected. What appears to be real and dangerous is made to look ridiculous or funny. For example, if one were to watch a man being blindfolded and tied to a post in front of a firing squad, it would obviously appear to be a serious and dangerous situation. Tension would most likely mount as members of the firing squad raised their guns and aimed them at the helpless man. If, however, instead of the crack of rifle fire, a silk flag with the word BANG on it popped out of each gun barrel, the unexpected ending might well produce a sudden tension reduction and a feeling of amusement. "The principal thing," Sigmund Freud contended, "is the intention which humour fulfills, whether it concerns the subject's self or other people. Its meaning is: 'Look here! This is all that this seemingly dangerous world amounts to. Child's play — the very thing to jest about!' "[6]

Those who are able to laugh at their own mistakes and failures are, other things being equal, inclined to be better adjusted emotionally than those who cannot. People who take themselves too seriously also tend to take life too seriously. They are apt to have a negative self-concept, and hence not be able to take failure lightly since it reinforces their already ingrained image of themselves as inadequate. Unable to laugh at themselves, they fear laughter by others as well. The tendency to deny and conceal their shortcomings is exaggerated and they become sensitive to criticism and rejection. To them, losing, errors, mistakes are deadly serious, not humorous. On the other hand, a mistake or failure we find funny can hardly be viewed as a tragedy.

While a negative self-concept may work against the likelihood that a person will laugh at his or her own misfortune, some theorists believe it to be a favorable characteristic for those who make a living taking humorous pot shots at others — the writers of satire. James Thurber, Robert Benchley, Lord Byron, and Mark Twain, among others, are thought to have hurled satirical barbs at society partly as a projection of their own negative feelings about themselves. Mark Twain, for example, wrote that Byron "despised the human race because he despised himself. I feel as Byron did, and for the same reason."[7]

One Person's Loss Is Another's Laugh

Much of what is considered humorous is disguised (or not so disguised) aggression. Wit, satire, parody, and sarcasm are all used to attack or ridicule persons, institutions, and society. It has long been known that one of the best ways to deflate a pompous, authoritarian ego is to turn the person into a laughingstock through well-directed humor. Charlie Chaplin's classic comedy *The Great Dictator,* for example, was designed to induce the American public to see Adolf Hitler during World War II as a laughable misfit rather than someone to be viewed with fear and awe.

Many of the world's great humorists and satirists are very angry individuals who vent their hostility through a clever manipulation of language. In so doing they also frequently alter the perception of their audience. The cutting words of Ambrose Bierce, who defined history as "an account, mostly false, of events, mostly unimportant, which are brought about by rulers, mostly knaves, and soldiers, mostly fools," have an impact not unlike the blade of a meat cleaver. And the irreverent blasts by the late comedian W. C. Fields, who immortalized such pronouncements as "Anyone who hates dogs and loves whiskey can't be all bad" and "I am free of all prejudices. I hate everyone equally" might be likened to a hit on the head with a baseball bat. Yet we laugh because the humorists have the audacity to attack our sacred institutions and conventions and help us see their imperfections.

The epitome of aggressive humor is found in slapstick comedy. When someone is hit in the face with a custard pie or falls into a swimming pool, or when Sylvester the Cat sticks his paw into an electric socket, the audience howls with laughter. It is especially hilarious if the victim is seen as a villain or as excessively pompous and stuffy. The butt of the joke in true slapstick comedy suffers primarily a loss of dignity, not serious or permanent physical harm. Since many of us have been the victims of this type of humiliation, either in reality or in our own self-denying fantasies, we relish the fact that it is now happening to someone else. Someone else is the loser, the helpless buffoon, and we thoroughly enjoy the sudden reversal of roles. Those who wind up with pie or egg on their faces are viewed as losers by the rest of us who now see ourselves transformed into winners. Humorist Will Rogers summed up the situation by stating, "Everything is funny as long as it is happening to somebody else."

Chapter 4

Striking Out
with the Bases Loaded

No one is a complete failure. Every living person succeeds at something — even if it is only to survive for one more day. While we all win and lose in different ways and at different times, there is often a *pattern* of successes and failures that reveals something about our basic personalities. One of these patterns is winning the unimportant battles and losing the big ones. Most people, of course, feel the increased pressure when the stakes of winning or losing are high, and many choke under extreme stress. The mind of a quiz show contestant may go blank when trying to think of the correct answer to the jackpot question. A baseball player, who has hit safely when it made little difference, may strike out with the bases loaded and two away when a hit would win the game.

The difference between a champion and others with superior talent is frequently the ability to come through under pressure, to make the big play when it really counts. There are many factors that make people tense and prevent them from doing their best under pressure. Surprisingly, however, some people seemingly go out of their way to fail when apparently they would gain the most by winning.

The Fear of Success

Everyone knows about the fear of failure. The dread of losing spurs some people on to greater effort; for others, it is a favorite excuse for not trying, for not competing. Less is known about the fear of success, although it is probably at least as prevalent.

People who are truly successful find themselves in a paradoxical situation. They are admired, treated with respect and deference, and given various rewards and honors. At the same time they find themselves envied and hated by many of those whom they have surpassed. Some people hover around winners because of their fame or their money but have no personal interest in them. Great accomplishments or wealth may create barriers to rewarding human relationships, so that successful people are apt to feel lonely, alienated, and isolated. Even the excessive attention and public exposure may prove uncomfortable or irritating. It is difficult to be both a winner and anonymous at the same time.

Being successful is also likely to carry with it a good deal of responsibility. Those who rise to positions of leadership are required to make more decisions and assume a bigger share of management burdens. Once people are identified as winners they are expected to continue to do better than others. Irving Berlin, the famous songwriter who gave the world such outstanding hits as "White Christmas" and "God Bless America," complained that "The toughest thing about success is that you've got to keep on being a success." The person who rises above the pack is not only expected to continue to excel but is constantly challenged by others for the role of leader. And it is not only true that the higher you rise the farther you have to fall, but that the higher you rise the more people there are who will cheer if you should make a downward plunge.

Although most of us desire the rewards of winning enough to try to obtain them in some fashion, there are many who become increasingly fearful and anxious as they near their goals. Either consciously or unconsciously they sense that they are approaching a crossroads. If they win, their lives will be changed significantly, and the change is anticipated as threatening. If the threat is perceived as too great, those who are afraid of success will choose not to win by finding some way to fail. It takes courage to assume the responsibility and face the pressures engendered by being singled out as superior. It also takes courage to defy the mores of the culture and say, "The cost of winning is too high and I'm not willing to pay it." Consequently, many people are caught in a conflict of unconsciously trying to fail while consciously struggling to win.

Goals may vary, and strategies for achieving those goals are many. The reasons given for failing are equally numerous, but only rarely does a person who loses because winning is more frightening admit to the fear, much less confess that the fear is responsible for losing.

Kathy Milner claimed the reason she had been unable to find a "deep and meaningful relationship," was that "all the men I meet are afraid of showing their emotions or making a commitment." Jeffry Arthur believed the only reason he had not yet made his millions on the stock market was that he still had not figured out exactly the right formula. Keith McCarthy blamed his inability to shed thirty pounds on an endocrine disturbance. And Merrilee Johnston was sure that when she finally found the right career, she would be a great success. Yet, all of them were hampered in their quests by an unreasonable fear of winning. They made progress toward achieving their goals until they were very close to winning. Then they choked and unconsciously did something to insure their own failure.

Kathy was an attractive, twenty-eight-year-old nurse. She had many friends and many dates but few serious involvements. She confided to a few of her closest friends that what she wanted more than anything was to "fall in love, get married, and have kids." Nearly all who knew her considered Kathy to be a very warm and friendly person. Few realized that behind her open and affectionate facade she was terrified of letting down her guard and trusting anyone with her deepest feelings. Whenever her defenses began to give way and she started to feel more than friendship for a man, she found some excuse to break off the relationship. She saw him as "too pushy," or "too possessive," or "only interested in sex"! But she was unaware that these were merely excuses to avoid intimacy.

Love is likely to be at or near the top of most people's list of needs and desires. For Kathy Milner, like millions of others, it was not only the most important but also the most frightening thing in her life. She had always been hungry for love, but had learned early in life to conceal this need because it was too painful to want something that badly and not have it. She knew her parents cared for her, but they were both inhibited in expressing their emotions openly. Although her hunger for affection remained because it had not been satisfied, Kathy's fear of vulnerability from loving and being loved set up an anxiety reaction. By breaking off any potentially serious love relationship, Kathy was able to dispel her anxiety before it became intolerable.

When Jeffry Arthur inherited some money from his father, he quit his job. Unlike his father, who was a hardworking, God-fearing man, Jeffry hated work and savored the thought of making "an easy buck." Jeffry liked to compare himself to Abraham Lincoln, and he memorized one of

Lincoln's little-known philosophical comments, "My father taught me to work, but not to love it. I never did like to work, and I don't deny it. I'd rather read, tell stories, crack jokes, laugh — anything but work."

After looking into a number of investment opportunities, Jeffry decided to try his hand at the stock market. He talked to people, read books, and subscribed to several of the leading market newsletters. He anticipated public opinion and world events astutely, and was able to make some shrewd investments. His capital grew substantially. Then, abandoning the sound principles and advice that he had used successfully until that time, he invested heavily in a poor risk speculation and lost most of his money. Undaunted, Jeffry started over. Gradually, he again built up his capital and again lost it by making another unwise decision.

Although he thought of himself as a hedonist and espoused the joys of easy living and quick money, these values were in conflict with the Puritanical training of his youth. The "virtues of hard work and thrift" drilled into him by his father remained unmodified in his unconscious, lying in wait to produce a sense of guilt whenever Jeffry deviated significantly from his early teachings. Since the guilt was not usually experienced consciously, however, it was not always recognized for what it was. It often manifested itself in disguised forms. One of these was the fear of success whenever Jeffry was on the verge of accumulating too much money too easily. Jeffry's fear of success was expressed in unconsciously motivated bad judgment at the crucial point, when such a decision would undermine an otherwise successful investment strategy. Small winnings were acceptable to his conscience, but he felt too guilty to win big without expending a lot of hard work and effort. By not winning Jeffry could avoid having to deal with an overwhelming sense of guilt.

Keith McCarthy bounced from one diet to another with about equal success. He tried grapefruit, liquid protein, and diet pills. He took up jogging and bicycling and the Air Force exercise program. He fasted and he counted calories. Everything worked for Keith — for a while. Five, ten, even fifteen pounds were lost regardless of what program he undertook. Never, however, could he take off enough weight to look as trim and athletic as he claimed he wanted to be. The closer he came to his ideal weight, the more difficulty he had in maintaining his current regimen, and the harder it became to ignore his compulsion to overeat. Each time he quit a diet and yielded to an eating binge, Keith rationalized that his weight problem stemmed from an endocrine imbalance and was beyond his control.

In reality, Keith felt extremely insecure in interpersonal relations, particularly when he was attracted to a woman. As long as he was fat, he believed himself unattractive to women and he was able to use that perception as an excuse to conceal his own sexual desires. As long as he felt physically unappealing, Keith was able to relax and relate to women in a friendly, jocular manner. The more weight he lost, however, the less fat he had to hide behind and the closer he came to having to deal with his underlying problem. On one occasion when he was close to approaching normal weight, a woman co-worker whistled at him appreciatively. "Wow, Tiger!" she purred seductively, "do you ever look sexy!" This so unnerved Keith that he rushed out and downed three hot dogs, a large Coke, a piece of pie, and a hot fudge sundae.

Merrilee Johnston, at thirty-two, had had almost as many jobs as Keith McCarthy had had diets. She had been a checker at a grocery store, a clerk in a law office, a research assistant in a cosmetic factory, and a customer representative for the telephone company. In between jobs she usually took classes in preparation for her next occupation. She didn't consider herself a job-hopper nor did she view herself as flighty or difficult to please. She was convinced that when she found the right career, she would not only stick with it but become very successful.

What Merrilee was not aware of was a pattern of behavior that led up to her quitting each position. Because she went out of her way to be agreeable and to please others, Merrilee was well liked by her employers and fellow workers. She never objected to working overtime or odd hours. Her work was always done carefully and on time. Rarely was she late for work and she never complained about wages or working conditions. She made coffee, sharpened pencils, and ran errands as if she enjoyed being of service. These characteristics did not go unnoticed.

The pay raises and the words of appreciation she received pleased Merrilee very much, and she was thrilled if her efforts won her a promotion. Things generally went downhill shortly after each advancement, however. She found herself losing interest in her job and thinking about a new career.

What lay behind her disillusionment with work was not the job itself, but the changing nature of her relationship with other employees because of the job. *She was no longer in a position to please everyone.* With each promotion she was required to make decisions that affected other employees, who would not always be happy with the results. Often she would have to give orders to others, put demands on their time, or criticize them for their inefficiency or mistakes. Running the risk of arousing their anger or disapproval placed a great strain on Merrilee and she would begin to have headaches and other somatic complaints. Rather than face the source of her discomfort — her need to be liked by everyone — she would lose interest in her job and begin preparing for a different line of work.

What Is Won by Not Winning

When fear of success is aroused sufficiently and the possibility of winning is in sight, something has to give. Either the person wins and experiences intense anxiety or other unpleasant feelings as the result of changes in his or her life, or the person does something to fail and hence reduces the threat of change. The threat may take many forms and will vary from person to person, but it is the reduction of threat that is the prize for losing. In most cases, however, the fear of success is all or partly unconscious, and it may stem from one or more of a variety of conditions.

Guilt

Guilt is a great equalizer. It is the undoing of kings and commoners, of business tycoons and welfare recipients. It is no respecter of age, sex, race, or socioeconomic status. Oedipus, the legendary king of Thebes, was driven by guilt to blind himself and give up his kingdom. Lady Macbeth suffered a mental breakdown, and her futile attempts to rid herself of guilt through compulsive hand washing are legendary. Skid rows are populated by alcoholics whose drinking excesses were triggered at least in part by guilt. Guilt feelings are a major factor in emotional depression, drug addiction, suicide, and other forms of self-punishment.

As with other emotions, guilt, in optimal amounts, serves a useful function. It prevents people from deviating too far from acceptable behavior, and thus allows them to function with little risk of serious punishment from society. What constitutes guilt-producing behavior varies as does the degree of guilt associated with such behavior. Guilt is learned from parents and other authority figures, and usually at an early age. It differs from person to person and from culture to culture. Sometimes guilt is excessive. It is frequently irrational, and often unconscious.

A person who deliberately lies, cheats, or steals may suffer conscious feelings of guilt for such an act. The guilt is self-imposed punishment for violating one's own set of moral values. If guilt is painful enough, the person may seek relief through atonement or forgiveness. Not infrequently, persons who have committed crimes confess because their guilt feelings are intolerable. Punishment by society is seen as preferable to their self-induced punishment.

When guilt is not experienced consciously, the criminal, instead of confessing, may unconsciously do something to insure being caught and punished. Such was the case of a very bright teenage delinquent. Despite an I.Q. in the 130s, his brief but otherwise successful crime spree ended when he was captured stealing hubcaps from a police car in, of all places, the parking lot behind the police station. Subsequent counseling revealed that part of the boy's delinquent behavior was motivated by a desire to call attention to himself because he felt unimportant and unloved. At first he felt smug and superior because he was able to pull off a series of petty thefts without getting caught. Before long, however, those feelings changed. He began to feel anxious and guilty about his illicit activities, and, as long as they went undetected, he could not receive the attention for his "cleverness" that he craved. His escapades finally became more daring and less intelligent until it was inevitable that he would get caught.

Guilt is not always related to something as tangible as stealing hubcaps. Frequently it is a nebulous, generalized feeling. Occasionally it is all-pervasive. Some people seem to feel guilty merely for breathing or being alive. Those who have an overabundance of guilt inevitably have a poor self-image. Their strong feelings of inferiority often cause them to become overly aggressive. If their assertive, competitive attempts to overcome inadequacy involve excessive drinking, bragging, cheating, or other unacceptable behavior, more guilt is added. Even when all the rules are followed, however, only a limited amount of success can be tolerated. If one feels guilty for breathing, being very successful would be unbearable.

An unconscious need to fail has been postulated as one of the contributing factors in compulsive gambling. It has been suggested that the reason the compulsive gambler cannot walk away from the game while winning is that winning makes the person feel guilty. That negative feeling persists until not only the winnings but the original stake is lost. By atoning for the sin of winning, the compulsive gambler may even feel elated by losing.

While these are extreme examples, guilt plays some role in the lives of everyone. The Puritan ethic, upon which American morals were originally founded, has not been totally eliminated as a viable force in the development of present-day character. And the mainstay of the Puritan ethic is the imposition of guilt feelings for any deviation from the acceptable code of behavior. Although success is highly prized in the American Puritan tradition, it is only valued when it comes as the result of hard work and the ability to overcome adversity, which is what develops "good character." Any shortcut to success is considered immoral since it limits the development of character, and character is deemed necessary to handle the responsibility that comes with success.

The business executive who rises to the top after a long apprenticeship or the athlete who wins a championship after years of preparation and training are generally admired and respected more than are those to whom success comes quickly. They are also more likely to adjust effectively to the demands and temptations resulting from the rewards of winning, such as acclaim, notoriety, status, and wealth. In contrast, many who win too easily or too quickly feel they do not deserve the rewards they receive for their minimal efforts. They feel guilty about achieving too much return for their limited investment and tend to lose, or at least stop trying to win more, in order to feel comfortable with themselves.

Envy

The more successful people become, the more likely they are to arouse the envy and hostility of others who have achieved less. Envy is often a spur to competitiveness and aggression. The envious person wants something of value that another person has and may be determined to go to great lengths to obtain it. The envious person is also most likely to sense the envy of others or to project his or her own envy onto others. In either case, the anticipated envy and corresponding hostility from other people, which results from one's own competitive efforts, may unconsciously interfere with the zeal for winning too much. If every success is perceived as arousing increased envy and aggression in others, winning can indeed seem dangerous even though highly desirable.

JoAnne had always been envious of her older sister. Donna was prettier, more popular, and a better student than JoAnne was. As far back as she could remember, JoAnne had lived in her sister's shadow, but for the most part she concealed her negative feelings. When she found herself hating Donna, she would deny it and tell herself she really loved her. In athletics, JoAnne showed great promise. Her gym teachers encouraged her to participate in swimming, tennis, and bowling, and she did very well in all of them. But she never did quite as well as her teachers and coaches believed her capable of doing. Although she wanted to succeed and to win recognition for her achievements, her fear of winning was even greater. It was rooted in her apprehension about the possible hostility from those she defeated. She unconsciously expected the same envy and hostility from them that she felt toward her sister.

Like so many negative emotions, envy is not always obvious. Because it is generally unacceptable to admit to being envious, most people try to deny or repress it. Many are so successful at concealing it that it goes undetected under normal conditions. The seventeenth-century philosopher Spinoza went so far as to say, "Those who are believed to be most abject and humble are usually most ambitious and envious." Consequently, when envy, or the fear of envy, inhibits one from going all out to win, and leads to a loss instead of a victory when the chips are down, the underlying psychological reason for defeat may be unknown to all concerned.

Alienation

Very successful people are likely to feel isolated and alienated from others. The person who rises to a position of power knows that success is tenuous and is maintained only through constant vigil. The dictator in a politically unstable country, the president of a large corporation, and the top box-office attraction in any field of entertainment learn to distrust anyone and everyone who might possibly depose them. When success involves a good deal of money, one cannot always be sure that friends, acquaintances, or lovers are not attracted primarily because of the money. The much-married billionaire J. Paul Getty was constantly besieged with offers of romance and marriage, and many of the proposals made it clear that these women were attracted more by the color of his money than the color of his eyes.[1]

The aura of success and power intimidates many people, and they shy away from those who possess it because it makes them feel uncomfortable. Others are attracted to winners, like moths to the flame. Yet meaningful relations and intimate friendships depend upon mutual trust, affection, and open lines of communication, characteristics which are often inconsistent with high levels of success. The more successful people become, the more their relationships tend to become *vertical*. Other people look up to them, and they look down on others. It becomes increasingly more difficult to find people to relate to on an equal, or *horizontal*, plane because obviously there are fewer people of similar stature with whom to relate.

The prime example of isolation and alienation from people as a result of extreme success is the late Howard Hughes. In his earlier years he parlayed a modest inheritance into a gigantic industrial empire. He was brilliant, talented, attractive to women, famous, and very wealthy. By every objective standard, Hughes was the epitome of success. Yet in his later years he became increasingly withdrawn and suspicious and spent the last years of his life in virtual isolation from the world.

While most of us profess a desire for fame, success, and riches, when the price we have to pay is isolation and alienation, the pay off may not be worth the cost. Either consciously or unconsciously, we may default or set ourselves up to lose because at some level, the "big win" is really perceived as more of a loss than a victory.

Self-Concept

Some people are afraid of success because it is inconsistent with their self-image. Even in fantasy they cannot imagine themselves becoming more successful than some predetermined level. Through a fluke or some extraneous circumstance, a person occasionally wins more than he or she ever thought possible, but in most cases people limit their successes to a level that will allow them to feel comfortable, a level that is consistent with their self-concept.

To reach your goal, whether it is to become a physician, a world-class chess player, or to break a hundred on the local golf course, you must choose not only a goal that is realistic in terms of your ability, but one that is also consistent with your self-image. Some people fall short because they strive for goals beyond their abilities to achieve, but others fail because they see themselves as inadequate, unworthy, inferior, or too insecure to handle a very successful role. On the verge of breaking par, such a person will unconsciously shank the ball into the rough or overshoot the green, thus eliminating the anxiety, embarrassment, and notoriety associated with achieving unexpected success.

Sexism

Traditionally the fear of success has been more prevalent among women than among men. This is especially true when there is competition between males and females and where success is dependent upon some degree of aggressiveness. It has not only been considered poor taste for a girl to beat her date at tennis or bowling, but it might also cast doubts on her femininity. Thus the satisfaction of winning would be offset by the possibility of social condemnation and the probability of no more dates with her male companion.

For males, on the other hand, success has been highly valued. Aggression and competitiveness have long been considered masculine traits, and social rejection for utilizing them in a winning effort would be unlikely under most conditions.

In recent years, as more attention has been given to social influence on the development of male and female roles, a few research studies have investigated the relation of sexual differences to the incidence of fear of success. Foremost is the work of psychologist Matina S. Horner, president of Radcliffe College, who found that 65 percent of female college students studied expressed fear of success when competing with men, as compared with only 9 percent of the males who competed against women.[2] The fear of negative consequences for success was greatest among those women who had high achievement goals and high levels of ability. Presumably the less ambitious, less competitive women showed less conflict and anxiety because they did not aspire to compete and win over their male counterparts.

In a subsequent study by two Australian psychologists, the incidence of fear of success among women was lower than in Horner's study.[3] They concluded that in addition to the differences in culture between the two samples, part of the discrepancy might be attributed to rapid social changes in the redefinition of sex roles and in attitudes toward traditional forms of success. As society moves away from rigid male-female stereotypes, fear of success will undoubtedly take on more of a unisexual characteristic and no longer will women have to go out of their way to lose so as to save face for their male opponents.

Chapter 5

Striking Out
with the Bases Empty

While some people try hard to win and manage to achieve small successes but never make the big time, there are others who never get out of the starting gate. They are sometimes known as "born losers," the people for whom losing is a way of life. Some people do well only when they are not under pressure, but chronic losers fail whether there is stress or not. Unlike those who lose because of a fear of success, a masochistic satisfaction, or some other psychological need, these people accept failure as inevitable, while making little effort to succeed.

In an issue of the humor magazine *Mad,* Born Losers were described as "always underfoot, waiting to get hit on the head by every misfortune the rest of the world drops." A Born Loser is "the one who rushes into traffic to rescue a confused puppy, and gets a ticket for jaywalking. He's the one whose car horn gets stuck just as he's beginning to make out in a drive-in movie . . . Born Losers never hear prowlers ransacking their living rooms because they're making too much racket upstairs installing burglar alarms. Born Losers starve themselves into malnutrition in order to afford the premiums on Health Insurance policies that cover every illness but malnutrition." [1]

We all know people who fit that mold — people who go through life achieving little and who seemingly are not too concerned about it. They appear to accept defeat or lack of success philosophically regardless of how many times they strike out. If we limit our discussion to those people whose failure syndrome is the result of psychological factors and exclude conditions over which they have no control, chronic losers still make up a sizable percentage of the population.

Fear of Change

While it is true that people can adjust to almost anything if change takes place slowly enough, all change demands something of the person involved. And the bigger or the more rapid the change, the greater is the demand. One of the advantages of learning a routine is that once learned, it can be carried out with little if any conscious thought. Habitual behavior requires no decisions. It is performed automatically and efficiently with a minimum expenditure of effort.

Change, on the other hand, requires decisions, trial-and-error behavior, and new ways of reaction. It involves risk and the unknown. Many people stay in a rut not only because it is easier, but also because they perceive it as safer. While a few see the unknown as an exciting challenge, more view it as a source of threat and danger. That which is familiar, on the other hand, makes us feel secure. Just as one person may hang on to an unsightly old pair of shoes because they are comfortable, another person may be unwilling to give up a lifestyle of losing. The comfort and security of the known is preferable for such individuals to the anxiety of the unknown, even when the known involves defeat. Whether the defeat involves poverty, unhappiness, loss of respect, or running last in a race is of secondary importance. If given a choice between a familiar pattern of loss and deprivation or the opportunity for acquiring success, a surprisingly large number of people will stick with the known pattern of failure.

An example of this phenomenon is found in Anton Chekov's famous short story "Kashtanka." [2] The protagonist, a dog by the name of Kashtanka, becomes separated from her master, who had physically and verbally abused her. She is ultimately taken in and cared for by a man who feeds her well and is kind and affectionate toward her. Eventually, however, Kashtanka meets up with her former master and willingly goes with him, presumably to spend the rest of her life being subjected to the type of abuse with which she is familiar.

The people who are most afraid of the unknown generally have *learned* to be so. They lack confidence in their ability to meet challenges and overcome unfamiliar obstacles. They do not have a backlog of successful experiences to rely on when faced with new problems. Consequently, having had a history of failure in similar situations, they lack both self-confidence and successful coping skills. These inadequacies then contribute to the probability of failure in subsequent encounters with the unknown, and a self-perpetuating cycle of fear and failure exists.

In order not to feel anxious and helpless, it is necessary for people to feel that they are in control of themselves and the situations in which they find themselves. In unknown situations, of course, control is impossible since we cannot control something that has no identity or substance. We cannot master it until we know more about it. A primary difference between those who look forward to change and those who fear it is that the former are convinced that within a reasonable time they can gain control over a situation, while the latter are afraid they cannot.

Clinical evidence indicates that the degree to which we need control and fear helplessness is largely the result of how we experienced our first human relationship, usually with our mothers, in infancy. Being dependent upon another person for the satisfaction of all of our needs can be rewarding, terrifying, or somewhere in between. Those who have learned in infancy that being helpless and dependent is frightening and unrewarding tend to see the world as threatening from that time on — unless something dramatic happens to change their perception. As adults they view every new situation with apprehension. Attending a cocktail party where they know no one and are not sure what is expected of them is anxiety-provoking. Changing jobs, moving, or any break from an established routine will be experienced as threatening. If people with this pattern of behavior have become accustomed to a lifestyle of failure and defeat, they, like Kashtanka, will be fearful of exchanging it for the possibility of something better.

Adaptation to Failure

Another deterrent to giving up an extended losing streak, and one that is partially related to a fear of change, is the ability to adjust to a life of failure. Some people are able to deal with losing without being overly frustrated or disappointed. They don't feel overwhelmed by loss. Not only do they learn to cope with defeat, but in some cases that is the one thing they do well. Since the only area in life in which they are successful is in handling the problems of losing, they are reluctant to give it up.

A patient who had been in psychotherapy for five months but who was making only minimal progress was finally forced to look at his resistance to change. He was locked into a miserable relationship with his wife, was on the verge of losing his job because of poor work habits, and consistently lost more money than he could afford to at the racetrack.

When confronted with his pattern of chronic failure, Alex Langdon reluctantly admitted that since he had been a failure all of his life, he had no illusions about winning. Anticipating failure in whatever he attempted, his expectations were usually borne out. There was a certain amount of satisfaction in knowing that whatever defeat he suffered, it would not overwhelm him. He knew what to expect and he could prepare himself for it. He could handle it. "Unlike the guy who hits himself over the head with a hammer because it feels so good when he stops," he explained, "I continue to hit myself because if I stopped I wouldn't know what to do with myself."

While the American tradition stresses that each generation should surpass the preceding one in education, opportunity, and standard of living, a large number of people never accept the challenge of upward mobility. Instead of striving for wealth and success, these people adapt to a condition of poverty and failure. Rather than working to become class valedictorians, they settle for being the class clowns. They learn to tolerate chronic misfortune and to carve out an existence that is as painless as possible. A part of that adjustment involves not setting goals that are too high and not trying too hard to succeed, since wanting something that they perceive to be impossible to attain leads to frustration and anguish. Although such an adjustment helps perpetuate a losing role, it may also make losing bearable.

Identification with Other Losers

A great deal of learning takes place by imitation. As children we learn to talk by imitating the sounds we hear others make. We learn to walk by observing our elders and by attempting to imitate their movements. Most of our attitudes and values are learned by introjecting qualities that are held by our parents and other significant individuals in our lives when we are young. If we happen to have models who themselves are failures, it is probable that we will adopt their losing attitudes and behavior.

In a ghetto, for instance, there are few successful models with whom to identify. Examples of poverty, unemployment, and other manifestations of failure, on the other hand, are plentiful. Under such conditions it is easy to learn what it is like to be a failure and to develop defeatist and pessimistic attitudes. Aspirations to become a lawyer, banker, or physician are hard to come by if one has never known anyone who follows one of those professions. The drive to become successful and to achieve is difficult to acquire if one is surrounded by people who are filled with despair and have resigned themselves to a life of failure.

Generally we tend to imitate the behavior of those people we admire. We are most likely to identify with the heroes and heroines in the movie rather than the villains. We like to be associated with the winners of athletic events, not with the losers.

As children, however, the persons we are most likely to identify with are our parents. Since this identification begins at an age before we are able to make very fine discriminations, we do not deliberately select the qualities we internalize from our parents. We don't decide to imitate Father's generosity and reject his bad temper. We take whatever is available, good and bad alike. While most parents would like to think that only their best characteristics are imitated by their children, such is not the case. A mother who overheard her daughter shouting at a group of neighbor children and ordering them about in a most arrogant manner reprimanded the girl for her bossy behavior. "But I have to," the daughter protested. "We were playing house, and I was the mother!"

Not only do we incorporate many of our parents' values and behavioral traits, but once they surface they are apt to be reinforced by other people. A son who shares his father's mechanical interests or a girl who imitates her mother's style of dress will most likely receive parental approval. If, on the other hand, the boy learns his father's tendency to brag or the daughter picks up her mother's habit of overspending, these traits are apt to arouse negative attention. Once the label, whether it be positive or negative, is applied, however, the child unconsciously makes an attempt to live up to it or down to it, as the case may be. The child who is called sweet will try to be sweet; the child who is called fat will continue to overeat.

The school psychologist said that Jim had difficulty learning because of severe anxiety and a very low self-concept. His teacher called him lazy, and fellow students thought of him as a troublemaker. His Little League coach claimed that Jim was not only dumb but had two left feet. His father swore that he was incorrigible and would turn into a juvenile delinquent, while his mother accused him of being just like his father.

With so many negative labels to live down to, it was no wonder that Jim was a chronic loser. No one in his family was a winner. His father was an alcoholic, his mother a hypochondriac, and his older brother was in jail for pushing drugs. Not only did Jim lack any winning models with whom to identify, he had a very low opinion of himself and no one expected or encouraged him to be anything other than a loser.

Fear of Failure

In the last chapter we showed how a fear of success can lead to failure. Paradoxically, the opposite condition, a fear of failure, can also lead to failure. It is true that some people are driven to win and to succeed because losing is so abhorrent to them. On the other hand, there are some for whom the idea of losing is so devastating that they are afraid to take chances. Losing for them is considered shameful and humiliating. Therefore, any risk, any competitive situation, is avoided. Such individuals procrastinate as long as possible when forced to make decisions, since there is the possibility that whatever choice they make might be the wrong one. By waiting, there is always the possibility that someone else or fate will make the decision, thereby relieving them of responsibility if the choice turns out to be the wrong one.

If fear of failure is excessive, we tend to avoid activities in which we are not too proficient. We eliminate the possibility of developing our skills because we are afraid of trying and not succeeding, thus leaving ourselves open for possible ridicule. In avoiding these avenues of potential pleasure and achievement, we restrict our interests and limit the range of activities in which we might ultimately be successful.

Because people who have an exaggerated fear of failure have such a low opinion of themselves, they are overly dependent upon others for guidance and direction as well as decision making. They are also dependent upon others for confirmation of their own self-worth. They seek reassurance and approval from others to a degree, but they spend considerably more effort in avoiding disapproval. Disapproval, humiliation, and rejection are associated with being wrong. Consequently, people who are overly fearful of failure seek to avoid responsibility for their mistakes. Research shows that they are not only more likely than the average person to blame their losses on forces beyond their control, but they also deny that their *successes* are due to their own efforts or ability.[3]

Thus, an excessive fear of failure leads to an inevitable trap. Success is not enjoyed because it is felt to be undeserved. It is attributed to luck or other external factors, and the person fully expects to fail the next time. If given positive feedback about a successful accomplishment, the individual is likely to deny it and point out all the ways that the job might have been done better. The denial of success is designed to lower the expectations of others so that future performances will not be judged by high standards and hence be considered failures when those standards are not met. Frequently, the person plagued by a fear of failure will deliberately fail in some endeavor in order to lower others' expectations. In an attempt to protect themselves from the humiliation of anticipated failures in the future, such individuals are willing to lose in the present.

In studying the origins of the fear of failure, two psychologists at the State University of New York at Albany, Richard Teevan and Paul McGhee, found that it is most likely to develop in children whose parents mete out punishment for failure but do not reward success. In such a family, "the child is likely to develop a negative attitude toward achievement and become motivated by his fear of the negative consequences of failure."[4]

The child's self-image as a failure is also frequently reinforced by exaggerated parental fears for the child's safety or health or ability to compete. Children who are continually reminded that they are too frail to play ball, that they might get hurt if they roller-skate, that they shouldn't expect to get as good grades as older siblings, or that they aren't old enough or strong enough to mow the lawn or shovel snow, learn to think of themselves as inferior. They assume that if their parents think they will fail, they must surely be inadequate.

Where traditional sex roles have been rigidly upheld, opportunities to participate in "masculine" activities were restricted to boys, and "feminine" activities to girls. Boys who were not proficient in aggressive, competitive sports were considered losers but were usually not encouraged to try their hands at flower arranging or playing the violin, where they might have great talent. Girls, on the other hand, have been discouraged from playing football and other aggressive sports and have been conditioned to become passive, conforming — to prepare for careers as nurses rather than doctors, secretaries rather than business executives. Deviation from accepted stereotypes made one feel like a traitor to one's own sex, and also a probable failure in one's new role.

In comparison to adults and older children, we all feel weak and small and ineffectual when we are young. How and to what extent we learn to overcome these feelings of inferiority largely determines our unique personality structure or "style of life," according to the theory of Alfred Adler. Adler, a psychiatrist who was a contemporary of Freud's, believed that everyone has not only some degree of inferiority feeling but also a compensatory striving toward a goal of superiority. He felt that people who become neurotic or mentally disturbed have developed faulty ways of coping with life. Partly through poor parental guidance, they try to conceal their feelings of inferiority. They strive for superiority over other people rather than striving to become competent in solving the problems of living. Adler thought of mental disturbances not as illnesses but as mistaken lifestyles, since they perpetuate feelings of inferiority. Neurotics are not considered sick, but failures. They are afraid to face reality because they cannot accept their inadequacies or responsibility for their actions. Although they may develop a wide variety of disabling symptoms, neurotics' symptoms are rewarding because they serve the purpose of allaying an underlying fear of defeat.

People who have a severe fear of failure set themselves up to lose not only in business, sports, and academia but also in human relations. Intimacy and deep involvement always involve risk and the possibility of hurt and rejection, the very characteristics that are most threatening to these individuals. Seeking to protect themselves in their involvement with others, people with an exaggerated fear of failure tend to be cool and aloof and unable to give of themselves. Their defensive, mechanistic performance is likely to turn other people off. No one feels at ease around them, and more likely than not their distrust and lack of feeling result in the rejection and failure they so desperately fear.

You're O.K., I'm Not So Hot

Eric Berne, the founder of Transactional Analysis whose ideas became known to millions of people through his incisive and often humorous discourses on human behavior in books such as *Games People Play*, believes that people are programmed to become winners or losers early in life.

> From earliest months, the child is taught not only what to do, but also what to see, hear, touch, think, and feel. And beyond that, he is also told whether to be a winner or a loser, and how his life will end. All these instructions are programmed into his mind and his brain just as firmly as though they were punch cards put into the bank of a computer. In later years, what he thinks of as his independence or his autonomy is merely his freedom to select certain cards, but for the most part the same old punch holes stay there that were put there at the beginning.[5]

According to Berne, although people like to feel they are autonomous and hence superior to other animals, they are in reality the most compliant of all. From birth, he believes, we are controlled, tamed, conditioned to obey and to do what we are told. Most animals are not. Our first masters are our parents, then teachers, bosses, government officials, and whoever else can grab us and tell us what to do. We are also subject to domination by an internalized life plan, or script, which we have learned by the age of five or six. Designed to last a lifetime, these scripts are based on childhood decisions and parental programming that are continuously reinforced.

Because of the way in which they have been programmed themselves, parents help their children to develop either winning or losing scripts. Parents who want or need their children to be losers will systematically train them to become failures and to feel inadequate in whatever they attempt. Their offspring will continually be reminded of their loser's role by admonitions such as, "Can't you ever learn to do it right?" "Why must you always be so slow?" "Here, let me do it for you!" "You'll never learn." "Wipe your nose." "Wash your face." "You drive me crazy!" "You're always underfoot." "Don't you have any friends?" "Why can't you behave like your cousin?"

At the same time children are thus indoctrinated, they are exposed to the losing scripts of their parents and possibly of their grandparents. The woman who got pregnant to fulfill her own mother's dire prediction, "had to" get married, and has been unhappy ever since may thoroughly indoctrinate her daughter about the misery of marriage, the unfaithfulness of men, and the disgustingness of sex. If the girl ever overcomes her dread of marriage enough to give it a try, she is sure to make a mess of it. Or take the father who throws his "lazy, no-good" son out of the house because he lies around all day watching television and getting loaded. For twenty years the father has been complaining about how hard it is to make it in the world of work. "It's a jungle out there. They'll eat you alive. I've worked like a slave and haven't had a promotion in fifteen years. And with an attitude like yours, you'd be lucky to last a week." Yet he sees no connection between his daily outbursts and the disinclination of his son, who believes him, to go out and be eaten alive.

By listening, an alert observer can often tell a winner from a loser very quickly. A winner is likely to say "I lost that time, but now I know what I did wrong." A loser will say "If only . . ." or "I should have . . ." or "Yes, but . . ." The best way to tell a winner from a loser according to Berne is that "A winner is a person who knows what he'll do next if he loses, but doesn't talk about it; a loser is one who doesn't know what he'll do if he loses, but talks about what he'll do if he wins. Thus, it takes only a few minutes of listening to pick out the winners and losers at a gambling table or a stockbroker's, in a domestic argument or in family therapy."[6]

How to Keep a Losing Streak Going

A football or basketball team that loses thirty or forty games in a row is not likely to go into the next game with a winning attitude. No amount of inspirational talk or pep rallies is likely to overcome the expectation of losing and the team's resignation to probable defeat. Repeated failure leads to pessimism. Therefore, whatever else contributes to defeat — limited ability, lack of experience, or poor coaching — is compounded by psychological factors that help perpetuate the losing cycle.

Families as well as athletic teams have losing streaks. In some cases a losing syndrome may continue within a given family generation after generation. A person born into such a family is almost predestined to become a failure. Failure models with which to identify are easily available. Adaptation to a losing way of life is easier than trying to buck the family tradition. A negative self-concept is presented on a platter. A losing script is being prepared for the person even before birth.

With the odds so stacked against a person born into a family with a long losing streak, it is a wonder that anyone ever overcomes the handicaps and becomes a winner, although some do. The chances of breaking out of the failure mold would be better if more losers married winners. Then the impact of losing would be diluted and a child would have some winners to emulate. But such is rarely the case. Winners tend to marry winners and perpetuate a winning cycle, while losers are inclined to marry losers and produce more losers. The cliché that "opposites attract" does not generally apply to the polarities of winning and losing. More often when it applies at all, it involves one type of loser being attracted to a different type of loser.

People are attracted to each other not so much by whether they are alike or different, but because they fulfill each other's emotional and psychological needs. If our needs are neurotic, we will seek out people who will satisfy those needs. Most likely they will be other neurotics, who also look to us to fulfill their needs. Losers do not ordinarily seek out successful individuals with whom to associate or become involved. Like water, people seek their own level. Chronic and severe losers find their level in insignificant jobs, skid rows, or welfare roles; in jails, brothels, and state mental hospitals. Chronic losers with less tragic scripts are scattered throughout society. But wherever they are found, they most likely feel attracted to and are comfortable with other losers. And it is out of this selection process that they tend to choose spouses with whom they have children, who in turn continue the losing traditions of both sides of the family.

Even those who transcend a losing script and manage to become successful despite the many obstacles are usually deeply influenced by their early losing experiences. Alfred Caplin grew up in abject poverty, lost a leg at the age of nine, was a school dropout, and for a while lived on the bum. Many years later, as a highly successful and well-paid humorist, public speaker, and cartoonist under the name of Al Capp, he claimed, "I'm still afraid I may not eat tomorrow. I'm frightened — I'll probably never stop being frightened." [7] And the character that Al Capp identified with the most in his famous cartoon strip was not Li'l Abner, but Joe Btfsplk, the little guy with the black cloud over his head.

Chapter 6

The Joy of Losing

Seeking pleasure and avoiding punishment motivate practically everything we do. Of the two, the avoidance of pain is probably the more basic. We eat because our stomachs send disturbing messages to our brains if we go too long without food. We get out of bed and go about our daily tasks each morning because our alarm clocks and our consciences make life unpleasant for us if we don't. Our survival is dependent upon a network of unpleasant physiological experiences being activated whenever our needs are not met. In fact, we would probably do very little in life if we were not dissatisfied with the status quo.

It was pointed out earlier that those who have developed an excessive fear of failure were, as children, punished for losing but not rewarded for winning. This pattern of discipline is more prevalent in our culture than is the reverse. Even though we have largely outgrown the era in which children were supposed to be seen and not heard, we still have a tendency to give them a larger dose of don'ts than dos in the process of trying to shape them to fit into adult society. Hence, our culture generally tends to reinforce nature's own priority by teaching children first to avoid pain and then to seek pleasure. Yet, there are many people who, through one form or another of mental gymnastics, manage not to avoid pain but to derive pleasure from it.

Masochism

When Sigmund Freud first used the term *masochism*, he was referring to those who were able to enjoy sexual orgasm only as a result of physical pain. The term was derived from the surname of the Austrian novelist Leopold von Sacher-Masoch, whose novels often depicted characters who derived sexual gratification from being whipped. (For some reason Masoch never became as well known as the Marquis de Sade, the French writer for whom sadism was named.)

The pairing of pain and pleasure, losing and winning, begins in childhood. Too often we are taught that whatever is pleasurable, whether it be masturbating or eating too much ice cream, is bad and that anything we do that is bad deserves punishment. Children who are punished every time they exhibit curiosity about their bodies or display any type of sexual interest learn to associate pleasurable sexual feelings with the anticipation of pain and punishment. By the time they learn to hide their sex play from their parents, they have developed strong feelings of guilt and shame, which cause them to punish themselves for their sexual feelings and behavior. Particularly during adolescence the sexual drive is apt to be stronger than the forces of inhibition. It is only after sexual climax that feelings of shame, guilt, and self-condemnation set in. With most people the punishment comes after the deed that provokes it. With people who are masochistic, however, the punishment comes first. Like a child who is rewarded with candy for having eaten spinach, the sexual masochist receives the reward of a sexual orgasm only after submitting to sufficient physical or mental suffering.

Because of traditional cultural roles, masochistic sexual behavior has most often been associated with women, while the stereotype of the aggressive male has linked sadism with men. Masochism is not restricted to women, however, nor is it necessarily related to passivity or weakness. Many very aggressive, power-oriented men are sexual masochists. In a study of the sexual behavior of male politicians, psychologist Sam Janus and psychiatrist Barbara Bess found that a surprisingly large number of these men sought out prostitutes who would inflict punishment on them. These researchers ask,

> Why should men who spend their lives in the pursuit of power subject themselves to sexual power games in which they invite punishment and even outright torture? The answer lies in the sad fact that the politician sees all of life as an exercise in power and punishment. Punishment is the common denominator of his experience, whether it is directed against other people, if he is stronger than they, or against himself in anger at not being able to overpower others.[1]

In addition to relieving feelings of guilt about their sexual desires through punishment, Janus and Bess found that these men received other psychological rewards from their masochistic rituals. They were able, for example, to turn humiliation, suffering, and defeat into a psychological victory by comparing themselves favorably with martyrs like Jesus Christ and proving to themselves that they were truly superior because they could take more punishment than ordinary men.

Psychic Masochism

Today, both in psychological and popular usage, the term masochism applies to a wide range of behavior. No longer is it restricted to pain associated with sexual activity. It now includes the whole spectrum of self-destructive behavior from which people derive some sort of gratification, either physical or psychological. Nonsexual self-inflicted punishment is often called psychic masochism or moral masochism.

As with sexual masochism, the payoff for psychic masochism is not always easy to comprehend. It is difficult to understand why a well-educated, highly respected surgeon or priest allows himself to become an alcoholic. Or why a man in New Jersey has been mugged eighty-three times and hospitalized more than twenty times from the attacks, yet still does not move out of the neighborhood. Or why a very bright, straight-A student suddenly goes blank during an important examination. Perhaps it is a little more understandable why a man in California threw up his hands and said, "I surrender," when stopped by a police officer for making an illegal turn. When the officer asked, "Surrender to what?" the driver admitted holding up a bank earlier in the day, although he had apparently until then made a successful getaway.

The aim of the psychic masochist is to turn every defeat into an ultimate victory by turning pain into pleasure. As a result of this feat, the masochist sets out to lose while appearing to struggle desperately to win. The late psychiatrist Edmund Bergler, who coined the term *psychic masochism* and who considered it the basic neurosis of our time, characterizes those who fall into this category as "injustice collectors."[2] They constantly complain about how they are misunderstood and mistreated. While developing an almost paranoid suspiciousness of others, they actually set up the conditions and the situations by which they will be persecuted. While they appear to be victims of a cruel and punishing world, they actually write the script and cast themselves in the loser's role in order to maintain control over their suffering.

Psychic masochism is found in its most extreme form among severely self-destructive individuals such as alcoholics, drug addicts, and compulsive gamblers. Even if they have high intelligence, excellent educations, high social status, respected families and jobs, they seem to be driven to destroy themselves and to lose all vestiges of success, love, money, and self-respect. Some of these individuals continue to lose until they hit rock bottom, spending the rest of their lives in a marginal existence. Others, however, bounce back after hitting the bottom and begin building a new life, only to destroy it later.

Masochistic behavior, whether sexual or psychic, is not a simple development. There are a number of interrelated factors that contribute to its evolvement.

Dependency

Individuals who become psychic masochists typically have exaggerated dependency needs stemming from childhood. Their parents were unable to help them prepare properly to function as independent adults since the parents were inclined to be immature and self-centered themselves. Having a pathological overconcern for themselves, the parents had only a limited awareness of the needs and feelings of their children. Since they demanded that their own needs and wishes be met by their children instead of the other way around, the children most often saw their parents as hostile toward them. The parents were never satisfied with what their children did for them, and, therefore, the children were made to feel inadequate and guilty rather than successful. Because their strivings for independence went unrewarded, psychic masochists often continue to view themselves as losers the rest of their lives, feeling as inadequate and dependent as their parents expected them to be.

Guilt

Excessive guilt about sexual and aggressive impulses is inevitably found in the character structure of masochists. Their willingness to accept punishment and defeat allows them to atone for what they consider to be unacceptable thoughts and behavior. Punishment reduces their feelings of guilt. Thus, they again feel purified and worthy of love and acceptance.

Aggression

When masochists feel frustrated and angry, they are inclined to turn their aggression on themselves instead of against others. Because of their excessive dependency needs, they are fearful of losing whatever signs of affection they do receive. Consequently, even if other people frustrate or humiliate them, masochists are likely to accept responsibility for such behavior and even feel guilty for having precipitated it. Therefore, they feel justified in inflicting self-punishment in order to lessen the feelings of guilt.

Narcissism

As children we are all narcissistic. We are concerned more with our own needs, desires, and pleasure than those of other people. In learning to relate effectively with others, part of this narcissism disappears and, ideally, by the time we are adults, narcissism gives way to mature love. However, children whose needs for affection are not met are not likely to give up self-love since there is nothing to replace it. Hence, they remain narcissistic.

The overt manifestation of self-love is usually discouraged by parents and society. It is especially discouraged by parents of psychic masochists, who themselves tend to be narcissistic but resent it in others. An adolescent girl in such a home might be ridiculed by her parents if she is found admiring herself in the mirror. If she explained that she was looking for blackheads or some other defect in her appearance, such viewing more likely would be tolerated, perhaps even encouraged. The girl eventually learns that it is permissible only to look at herself in a negative way. Being ugly is rewarded while being pretty is not.

Many psychic masochists learn to exaggerate their awkwardness and make themselves the butt of jokes, gladly suffering derision and humiliation in order to bring attention to themselves and thus satisfy their narcissistic and exhibitionistic tendencies. Children who chronically misbehave in school often seek punishment for their behavior in order to receive attention and recognition from teachers and classmates.

Persecution

Psychic masochists have a history of feeling persecuted. In the process of becoming socialized, every child must learn to deal with frustration. Needs and desires cannot always be satisfied immediately. The rules of reality and society must be adhered to most of the time. The child who feels persecuted, however, experiences something far more traumatic than frustration. The child's feelings include suffering and humiliation at the hands of someone else — usually someone bigger and more powerful, most often a parent.

A parent who physically or psychologically abuses a son or daughter may well produce a passive, dependent child with an extremely negative self-image. Sometimes the abuse is followed by protestations of love. When that is the case, a child may be willing to suffer continued defeat and degradation in order to win the perverted affection of the parent or subsequent parent substitutes. This is particularly true when persecution is executed under the guise of love, or for the child's "own good." Even battered children cling tenaciously to parents who burn their hands and break their bones.

Need for Control

The most terrifying experience most of us can imagine is to be completely helpless in the face of impending danger. In old-fashioned melodramas this was depicted by the heroine being bound by the villain and tied to the railroad track in the path of an oncoming train. The audience could usually identify with her fear, even knowing that she would be rescued by the hero at the last moment.

Because of their limited physical strength and lack of experience, children often feel helpless. However, most develop ingenious ways of dealing with the anxiety helplessness engenders. They turn to fantasy and see themselves as more powerful and capable than they really are. They learn skills and develop knowledge that provide a sense of mastery. They identify with adults who are more powerful. Therefore, rather than being at the mercy of others, they experience the power as being their own and under their own control.

As children, if our needs are not met, we are faced with two choices. Either we perceive that our parents are unable or unwilling to satisfy our needs — in which case we feel helpless, frightened, and unable to change or predict our fate. Or we can assume the fault is our own. Although this may lead to feelings of inadequacy, guilt, and failure, at least it provides us with a sense of being able to change our behavior and maintain some feeling of control over our destiny. By trying harder, by becoming more deserving, by improving our shortcomings, someday we will surely have our needs met. Psychic masochists, among others, tend to make the latter choice. They prefer to feel unworthy and guilty rather than helpless.

Another means of effecting a feeling of control over one's threatening environment is to regress to a state of infantile omnipotence. At birth infants tend to perceive themselves and the world around them as one and the same. They have a kind of megalomania, in which they see themselves as the center of the universe and able to command it to satisfy their needs. Before long, however, the infant begins to develop a vague awareness that the reverse is true. Rather than being omnipotent, the infant is really helpless and dependent on others for survival. The child whose needs are not met and who finds dependency overly threatening may seek to overcome the anxiety of helplessness by regressing to the earlier stage of infantile omnipotence. This is typical of those who become psychic masochists.

The problem with regressing to omnipotence is that it involves a denial of reality. It is really a delusion and like all delusions, it needs periodic reinforcement to keep it going. Therefore, the more pain and suffering that is endured, the greater the loss short of actual death, the more the masochist can say, "See, I am truly omnipotent. No one could suffer as much as I have and survive unless they are indestructible. Like the phoenix, I emerge from the ashes and rise again. This proves I am immortal!" The psychic masochist does not suffer pain and loss simply because it is enjoyable. Rather, *the joy is in surviving defeat and thus reinforcing the delusion of omnipotence,* which in turn temporarily reduces the terror of helplessness and vulnerability.

Tony was a thirty-eight-year-old alcoholic. His wife had divorced him and moved to another state with their two children. Over a period of time he had lost his job as a corporation pilot, his house, and his savings as well as his marriage. Periodically Tony sought help through Alcoholics Anonymous, a minister, and a number of counselors. He seemed to make progress for a while and then would quit, usually by going on a drunk. On one occasion he came close to developing insight into his delusion of omnipotence. He told the counselor that he sometimes worked for a friend as a crop duster. "The only time I really feel alive," he said, "is when I'm flying a few feet off the ground with sulfur pouring out the back of the plane. One spark from the exhaust and it's curtains! Challenging death and winning is really where it's at! When I put the plane down, I feel invigorated. I'm alive! Unfortunately, it doesn't last." Most of the time Tony was unaware of what was behind his self-destructive behavior. He did know, however, that when things were going well he became anxious and that after a certain amount of suffering he felt better.

A masochist's need for mastery can be seen in the contractual arrangements the person makes with those who apply the pain and suffering. A careful investigation usually reveals that a masochist, in order to find gratification from suffering, must set up the conditions and the personnel involved in carrying out the act. Although the illusion of being a helpless victim is part of the scenario, the masochist actually has precipitated the punishment that the sadist delivers. Unprovoked suffering does not have the desired effect. By writing, directing, and casting the script the masochist maintains complete control over the whole production, thus *undoing* the real helplessness that was experienced in childhood.

The senator who pays a prostitute to tie him up and whip him and the battered wife who dares her husband to hit her even though she has been previously hospitalized a dozen times for similar beatings can hardly be considered innocent victims.

You'll Be Sorry!

The classical retort of the child who has been punished for some wrongdoing, "You'll be sorry when I'm dead!," has many variations as a means of striking back at people who frustrate us. This mode of attack is sometimes called passive-aggressive behavior since it is indirect and sometimes rather subtle. Frequently, children who are afraid to express their aggression overtly and directly for fear of retaliation or loss of love learn to do so passively and indirectly. They often continue doing so into adulthood.

The aim of passive-aggressive behavior is to make one's tormentor suffer, usually through feelings of guilt. Persons who use this ploy are generally willing to suffer great losses themselves in order to achieve their revenge. Some go so far as to commit suicide in order to punish those they accuse of mistreating them. Revenge may be sweet, but for passive-aggressive people the price is often very high. Just as a masochist may secretly enjoy the distress experienced by the person who is maneuvered into inflicting punishment, and the stutterer may derive hidden satisfaction from observing the discomfort of those who are forced to listen, passive-aggressive persons are willing to take ten blows for every one they return.

Wilbur Donaldson was an elementary-school principal. He had a reputation for being a strict disciplinarian and he administered both his school and his home in a rigid, authoritarian manner. Billy, his only son, was expected to act like a little gentleman at all times and to do his chores promptly and with no excuses or complaints. In school Billy was shy and quiet and never caused trouble. He scored high on intelligence tests and occasionally showed signs of intellectual brilliance in class. However, Billy was a poor reader. He was put in special reading classes and given private tutoring, but to no avail. He gave the appearance of trying and he spent hours struggling over reading assignments, but each year he fell farther and farther behind his classmates in reading.

Like many other poor readers of average or above average intelligence, Billy unconsciously used his seeming inability to read as a means of rebelling against authority — in this case primarily his father and then his teachers and the school system. Although his teachers were frustrated and sometimes felt incompetent because they failed to teach such a bright child to read, they also had other problems and other students to worry about. Usually by a week into summer vacation, they forgot about Billy. Billy's father was alternately frustrated, angry, and disgusted. Billy was afraid to rebel against his father overtly and his father, being a school principal, was humiliated by his son's academic failure, but the price Billy paid for his revenge was to suffer the rest of his life because of his limited ability to read.

The parent who chooses the role of an invalid to control the family, the wife who constantly complains of poverty and of how difficult her life is in order to make her husband feel like a failure, the child who develops a fever every time she is scolded by her mother, and the worker who risks his job by working slowly in order to make his supervisor look bad are all using passive, indirect ways to express their aggression. In the process they accept the role of loser and suffer excessively in order to punish others for their real or imagined transgressions.

Martyrs and Other Heroes

Unlike masochists and others who deliberately subject themselves to loss and suffering, martyrs do not seek punishment.

However, they are so dedicated to a cause or a faith that, if necessary, they will endure suffering or death rather than renounce it. Religious martyrs are held up by their followers as examples of faith and courage. Many Christian martyrs, most notably Joan of Arc, have been elevated to sainthood by the Roman Catholic Church. Political martyrs and revolutionaries are sometimes driven as much by a desire for personal glory as by dedication to a cause. Observing this, George Bernard Shaw once remarked, "Martyrdom is the only way in which man can become famous without ability."

Heroes, in contrast to martyrs, risk their lives for other people rather than for abstract causes. The passerby who rushes into a burning house to save the occupants, the soldier who throws himself on a live hand grenade to protect his fellow soldiers, and the woman who dashes into the street to grab a neighbor's child from the path of an oncoming car are considered heroes. None of these acts is premeditated. In many cases heroes risk their lives for strangers they have never seen before and for no observable reward or reinforcement. It is a spontaneous act, done with little if any conscious thought. Heroic people see something to be done and they do it. Even afterward, heroes are often unable to give a more profound reason for their actions, or explain why they were willing to risk pain, injury, or loss of life by their heroic deeds.

The willingness to suffer is not restricted to a handful of martyrs and heroes. Physical fitness devotees jog endless agonizing miles, and millions of people endure great physical and psychic pain, exercising and starving themselves, for the cause of physical attractiveness. Many parents become martyrs. They somehow believe that is part of the parental role. The great success of Mell Lazarus' comic strip "Momma" can be attributed to the fact that so many people identify either with the hypochondriacal mother or her children who are made to feel guilty by Momma's antics. Lazarus claims he patterned Momma after his own mother. "In her mind my mother has been dying of a terminal illness for thirty-five years," he said. Mrs. Lazarus denied she was the model, however. "Many mothers are this way," she concluded. "It can't be me, it must be my sister Helen." [3]

In his best-selling book *How to Be a Jewish Mother,* Dan Greenburg gives some practical advice on how to manipulate people through the technique of self-sacrifice and how to turn defeat into psychological triumph over others by making them feel guilty. On the art of basic suffering, Greenburg recommends the following:

> To master the Technique of Basic Suffering you should begin with an intensive study of the Dristan commercials on television. Pay particular attention to the face of the actor who has not yet taken Dristan.
>
> Note the squint of the eyes, the furrow of the brow, the downward curve of the lips — the pained expression which can only come from eight undrained sinus cavities or severe gastritis.
>
> This is the Basic Facial Expression. Learn it well. Practice it before a mirror several times a day. If someone should catch you at it and ask what you are doing, say:
>
> "I'm fine, it's nothing at all, it will go away."
>
> This should be said softly but audibly, should imply suffering without expressing it openly. When properly executed, this is the Basic Tone of Voice. [4]

Greenburg points out that one does not have to be either Jewish or a mother to be a Jewish mother. An Irish waitress or an Italian barber could also be a Jewish mother.

A good Jewish mother believes that all of the world's ills can be solved by a bowl of chicken soup. Anyone who rejects her food is also rejecting her as a person, and she would die of shame if her children or guests went hungry. Institutions and governments sometimes feel the same way. Therefore, prisoners and other martyrs frequently go on hunger strikes to call attention to their causes, hoping to force those in power to adhere to their demands. After all, if these people died of starvation, what would the neighbors say? People who are prone to feel guilty are easily manipulated by those who are willing to sacrifice and suffer to get their own way.

Pay Now, Enjoy Later

One of the primary characteristics that distinguishes the mature person from the immature is the ability to put off immediate gratification in favor of long-term rewards. If you ask small children whether they would rather have one piece of candy now or five pieces tomorrow, most would probably take one now. Time seems endless to children and the basic tendency is to seek immediate gratification. As adults, on the other hand, we learn that we can ultimately achieve more if we first spend time, money, and effort preparing for our goals. We cannot spend all the money we make as soon as we get it and still have enough for a down payment on a house or car. We learn to put off, to make do, to do without. In doing so, we find that there is likely to be a bigger payoff in the future.

Carried to the extreme, however, it is possible for people to attribute value to suffering or deprivation itself rather than the ultimate reward. Many individuals who deny themselves comfort or pleasure for years in order to live well when they retire become so indoctrinated with the virtue of scrimping and saving that they are unable to change their habits even though they could well afford to do so. Some people actually compete with each other to see who has suffered the greatest hardships and lost the most. At meetings of Alcoholics Anonymous, group therapy sessions, and similar situations in which people share their problems and gain mutual support, an unconscious rivalry often takes place. Competition is in terms of who has had the toughest life and become the biggest failure. The prize is the respect and admiration of the group for having *survived* such an ordeal, perhaps more than for having had the courage to confess it to the group.

Pleasure extracted from misery and suffering is often enhanced by keeping it concealed from others. "If they only knew how much I am suffering . . ." is the theme song of those who suffer in silence. The "nobility" of suffering is thus enhanced by the fantasy that the sufferer would receive even more approval from friends and family for remaining silent. At times, though, people who suffer in silence feel compelled to let others know they are suffering in silence. While still pretending that their vow to secrecy is maintained, they manage to let their suffering be known. Because the fantasy is not sufficiently rewarding, sufferers need other people to appreciate their "bravery."

In times past, political and religious leaders have found it possible to keep the downtrodden pacified and free from revolutionary ideas by convincing them that not only was there personal satisfaction to be gained from hard, unrewarding labor but that suffering was pleasing to God. If the masses believed that the reward for pain and misery would come only in the hereafter, they would be willing to spend their lives demanding few if any earthly pleasures. They would even feel virtuous about suffering because the more they endured in life, the greater would be their reward in heaven.

By whatever method or for whatever reason people are

able to turn loss into victory, suffering into pleasure, one thing should be remembered. Martyrdom and masochistic behavior are learned. They are learned because in some way they are rewarding. There is always a payoff, although it may not be readily apparent. People do not continue to be self-destructive over a period of time unless the behavior, despite pain or humiliation, satisfies some important need or desire.

Chapter 7

Heads You Win,
Tails I Lose

While winning is usually more difficult than losing, there are times when winning is impossible. Phrases like "I'm caught between the devil and the deep blue sea" and "between a rock and a hard place" were invented to describe this kind of no-win situation. When faced with two or more choices, both or all of which are negative, there is no way you can pick a winner. The best you can do is to choose the alternative that is the least painful or costs the least in time, energy, or money. This is called a double-avoidant conflict. You may be struggling valiantly to maintain a rigid diet but are tempted by a hot fudge sundae. You either blow the diet or lose out on the pleasure that your taste buds are clamoring for. Students are continually faced with the unpleasant choice of either studying for or failing a forthcoming exam. For a kickback an important contract can be landed. The question then becomes, what is more important — a big contract or one's integrity?

No-win situations are more numerous than we sometimes think. We run into them many times a day. Some are so insignificant that we are apt to take them in stride, suffering only a temporary annoyance, while others can have a serious impact on our lives.

When James Freeman made an appointment to see a psychologist, he was a defeated man. Although he was vice president of a large manufacturing company, lived in the best section of town, and was given a distinguished service award by the chamber of commerce, James Freeman was depressed. He told the psychologist that life no longer had any meaning for him and that he saw no value in any of his accomplishments.

When they were young, Freeman and his wife had looked forward to the day when business success would provide them with the time and money to enjoy themselves and each other fully. They accepted the demanding hours of Freeman's job with the hope that someday they would reach their goal. As Freeman progressed on the job, however, his hours got longer instead of shorter, and he became more and more involved in his work and less and less interested in his family. Because she felt rejected by her husband, Mrs. Freeman began drinking excessively and, even though frustrated sexually herself, was rarely responsive to him. When he was home, they argued about his never being home. When he was at work, he felt guilty about being there. His unhappiness at home made him less effective at work, which made him spend even more time at his job. Clearly the demands of work and the demands of his wife were incompatible. And he was learning to dislike them both, as well as himself.

Although less true today than in the past, some women may still find themselves in what was once a classic conflict situation when they compete with men — especially in athletics, but also sometimes academically or on the job. If a woman fails, she not only experiences the letdown of the loss but may also feel a sense of self-betrayal if she did not perform to the best of her ability for fear of defeating her male opponent. On the other hand, if she wins she is afraid she will lose her popularity and femininity.

Double-Avoidant Conflicts and
Impractical Solutions

In most cases when a person is forced to choose between undesirable alternatives, the option representing the least loss is chosen. Faced with the choice of losing either a castle or a bishop, a chess player must decide which is the "lesser of two evils." A boy may agree to lose an hour of play time and spend it cleaning his room rather than face the wrath of his mother. A teenage girl may have to decide whether it is worse to stay home alone on Friday night or go on a date with a boy she dislikes. In some cases, however, the choices are perceived as so nearly equal and so equally threatening that the person is unable to make a choice. If the pressure to make a decision is great, anxiety increases as the time for making it grows near. Rather than deciding on one of the available unacceptable choices, some individuals, in order to dispel anxiety, literally or psychologically flee the scene and avoid making any decision.

A soldier afraid of being killed or wounded in combat, but equally afraid of being thought a coward by his fellow soldiers or himself, unconsciously developed a paralyzed arm and managed to get transferred to a hospital. A woman who really didn't want to get married, but who was unable to admit it to herself or to confront her fiancé and family, disappeared. She moved to another part of the country and took on a new name and identity — all on the basis of unconscious motivation. Having complete amnesia for her past life, she was unaware of the conflict she had left unresolved. Another woman, because of unresolved emotional and sexual problems with her husband, was seriously contemplating divorce. However, she was terrified of being on her own and having to take responsibility for her life. During the struggle to decide whether to go or stay, she developed a severe lumbar strain, which necessitated a prolonged hospital stay.

In these and similar situations, people can avoid making a tough decision, at least temporarily, by removing themselves from the scene or incapacitating themselves to the point where the decision is no longer relevant. The soldier who cannot hold a gun cannot be expected to go into combat. The wife who has a severe backache cannot be expected to have sex and she cannot walk away from her marriage. The unconscious takes over and provides an escape from anxiety caused by the conflict, although nothing is done to resolve the basic problem.

The amount of trauma involved in losing is dependent upon the value one puts on that which is lost. The loss of twenty dollars may be painful, but ordinarily it is nothing compared to the loss of life. Also, being faced with the choice of losing one or the other does not represent much of a conflict. There is no real basis for indecision. Unless, of course, you are like the tightwad depicted by the late, great Jack Benny. In one of his most famous skits, Benny was accosted by a holdup man who demanded his money. After a prolonged period of time, Benny had still made no move to hand over his wallet. The impatient robber then demanded, "Hurry up! Your money or your life!" Whereupon Benny, in deep thought, replied, "I'm thinking! I'm thinking!"

In addition to the threat of loss and the frustration of being caught in double-avoidant situations, apprehension and destructive potential increase if the person or persons making impossible demands are emotionally important to the individual who is in the middle. This happens frequently with children who are the victims of parents who impose conflicting value systems on them or parents who countermand each other's orders.

George and Alice have been married for nearly twenty

years. They view their marriage as nearly ideal. They claim
they never argue and rarely disagree. Their children, however, are frequently out of hand, and neither George nor
Alice has the slightest idea why. After a week's visit,
George's sister could have shed some light on the problem.
The following are some of the conflicting messages she had
heard her brother and his wife give their children:

George: "Dennis, get down here right now! Dinner is on
the table."

Alice: "Dennis, how can you come to the table with such
filthy hands and your hair uncombed?"

Alice: "If there is one thing I detest, it's doing house-
work. I hope you will learn a career, Wendy, and not become just a housewife as I am."

George: "I hope you don't listen to that Women's Lib
nonsense, Wendy. The only happy women are those who
stay home and take care of their homes and their children.
Women are not cut out for the battles of the business
world."

George: "Wendy, that creep with the long hair who
brought you home the other night. Are you sure he's not
some kind of fruitcake?"

Alice: "I'm glad you're going out with a nice boy for a
change. He's so well mannered. Not like some of those
rough characters that used to hang around."

Alice: "Dennis, why didn't you tell me you didn't have
money to go to the concert with your friends? You know I
would have given you some!"

George: "When I was a boy parents didn't spoil their kids
the way they do today. We had to earn every dime we got.
It wasn't doled out to us for every silly whim we had. We
learned the value of a dollar!"

Binds and Double-Binds

No-win situations in which one person gives another two contradictory messages at the same time have received considerable attention in recent years by psychologists and psychiatrists as well as by experts in communication theory. Known as double-bind communication, the conflict experienced by a recipient of a sufficient number of such messages frequently leads to severe emotional upset and pathological behavior. Double-bind commands given by parents are said to produce schizophrenic children and juvenile delinquents. A mother who bemoans her daughter's obesity while serving her a double helping of pie à la mode puts the girl in an untenable situation. A father who preaches law and order while exceeding the speed limit and telling his son to watch out for pursuing police cars presents mutually contradictory messages to the boy. Faced with a continuous barrage of double-bind conflicts from their parents, these children suffer an insoluble dilemma. In desperation, they either withdraw into a world of fantasy or act out their frustration in antisocial behavior. Even normal adults, when placed in experimentally induced double-bind situations, experience a significant increase in anxiety.[1]

When confronted with an expert in double-bind communication, we not only feel frustration, we are often unsure as to why we are upset. We have that disconcerted feeling of being victimized without knowing for sure how it came about. It is not unlike sparring with an opponent while blindfolded. Not only do you not know where the next blow is coming from, but neither do you know what effect your counterattack has on your adversary.

The essence of the double-bind message is to countermand every order — do with don't, yes with no, hurry up but wait. A master of the art, a mother who had contributed significantly to her son's inability to cope effectively with life, wrote him the following letter:

Dearest Greg:

Just a few lines to let you know I am thinking of you even if you haven't had time to write. I did appreciate your phone call last night, however.

I know you and your dad didn't get along too well last time you were home, but try not to think of the trouble. It's best to forget those things.

Don't let the cigarette habit get the best of you, Greg. You know how hard it is for you to resist temptation. I sent you a carton today, but you know that too much smoking isn't good for you.

I hope you're not worrying about your exams. With your brains you can pass them with your eyes shut. But if for some reason you don't, don't be upset. At least you tried, and that's all we can ask.

Write soon,
Mother

Parents are not the only experts in double-bind communication. Employers, schoolteachers, and lawyers are often proficient. Many government employees have developed it into a fine art. One family who wished to turn an existing garage into a rumpus room and build a swimming pool applied to the city building department for permission. They received a letter indicating a list of conditions that would be necessary in order to meet the city's building regulations. The conditions were, in part, as follows:

1. Enlarge the windows on the east side of garage.
2. Replace overhead garage door with wood siding.
3. Change the pitch of garage roof to conform to code.
4. Widen doorway from garage to rear yard and extend overhang 18 inches.
5. Tear down garage.

We are all familiar with local governments' home beautification programs, which encourage us to improve the appearance of our houses and make the neighborhood a more attractive place to live. And then they increase our property taxes when we comply.

What happened to Jim Hoover of Costa Mesa, California, is even more bizarre. The state-maintained roadway that fronts his printing shop was a weed-choked strip of dirt that had long been in need of a face-lift. So, good citizen that he was, Hoover decided to do his bit for local beautification. He bought forty dollars' worth of soil and spent another thirty dollars on plants. While he was in the process of sprucing up the parkway, an official of the state's department of transportation stopped and inquired if he had a permit to landscape the strip. The only problem in obtaining one, Hoover learned, was that the state does not give permits to private citizens. The reason, he was told, was that a private citizen might not maintain the new landscaping and it might revert to a weed-choked parkway — the way it was before. The official informed him that he would have to get a permit from the city. City bureaucrats refused to issue a permit, however. They said they did not want to be liable if Hoover did not maintain the landscaping. To make matters worse, the state issued Hoover a warning that he would be fined ten dollars a day if he did not remove his beautification efforts.[2]

The federal Meat Inspection Service ordered the Armour meat-packing plant to create an aperture in a sausage conveyor line so that inspectors could take out samples to test. The company complied. However, the Occupational Safety and Health Administration demanded that the aperture be closed as it was a safety hazard. "Each federal agency threatened to shut down the plant if it did not comply instantly with its order."[3]

Many children, especially precocious ones, learn early in

life to put their parents in double-bind situations. It is not uncommon for a child who bullies his little brother to make his parents feel guilty for punishing him by implying that the younger child started the fight. Or the younger one can instigate the trouble in order to win attention from the parents and see the older brother punished. Whatever they do, the parents are likely to wind up feeling like losers because they have the uneasy feeling that no matter which child they punish it is probably the wrong one.

Another double-bind conflict that parents often find themselves in is, "Mother, will you please stop nagging at me! I heard you the first time!" But if Mother stops "nagging" and only makes the request or the demand once, the task will be left undone. Poor Mother winds up being a bitch or doing the job herself.

How to Recognize a Double-Bind Trap

While people may feel anxious and trapped for many reasons, these negative feelings are also the first signs that one is caught in a double-bind situation. The target of a double-bind conflict believes that there is a correct response to the demand being made, and that if he or she only tries hard enough or is smart enough, the right answer can be found. Obviously that is not true, but the harder the person struggles to find the elusive winning solution, the more frustration will be evident.

Because of their frustration and inability to perform in a manner pleasing to the other person, victims of double-bind communication tend to view themselves as weak and ineffectual. No matter what they try, it doesn't work. They wind up feeling impotent and helpless because they don't know how the deck got stacked against them. Even venting their anger is futile because, as the father says while beating his son, "This is for your own good!" Direct attack on the perpetrator of the double-bind conflict seems inappropriate since the communication is usually disguised as concern or benevolence rather than as a means of domination and control. Victimized individuals may feel that they have been outsmarted, but they would feel even more foolish if they expressed their anger at someone who supposedly was concerned about them. The predicament is epitomized by the story of the mother who bought her son two ties for his birthday. To show his appreciation, the son wore one of the ties the next time he saw his mother. The mother's response, however, was, "What's the matter? Don't you like the other one?" [4]

The more the target of double-bind communication views the other person as superior or dominant or in control of the situation, the more difficult it is for that targeted person to be objective in evaluating the interaction. If we feel dependent upon the person who traps us in double-bind conflicts or if we are fearful of arousing that person's displeasure, we are likely to withdraw, become more passive, and assume unrealistic guilt for not being able to come up with the correct response or behavior. Our needs blind us to the reality of the relationship. The only way to break out of a double-bind trap is to realize that what appears to be a cooperative endeavor masks an underlying competitive struggle for dominance. Those who master the double-bind technique are like gamblers who play with a marked deck of cards. The game may appear friendly on the surface, but the eventual winner is never in doubt. We may lose innocently until we realize we are up against a card sharp, but if we continue to play after we know the nature of our opponent, we have no one to blame for our losses but ourselves.

Chapter 8

When Lady Luck Frowns

In Sutton Coldfield, England, a young free-fall parachutist was to be a star of the Rugby Carnival. However, he missed the target and landed on a high-voltage electricity pylon. A helicopter sent to rescue him caught its rotor arm in his parachute harness and sent him plummeting downward a hundred feet. Seeing his plight, rescuers gathered up a sheet and were prepared to catch him, but a gust of wind blew him away and he landed on the ground.[1]

Three Euclid, Ohio, high-school students decided to skip school and go on a picnic. They packed some canned spaghetti and a little marijuana and headed for the woods. Before long, however, they were surrounded by four police attack dogs and charged with possession of marijuana. It seems their picnic site was the area police used for training search dogs.[2]

Five persons were caught stealing during a softball game in San Fernando, California. They weren't players, though. They were robbers. After taking approximately $600 from a nearby ice company, they fled on foot past the softball diamond, jumped into their car, and took off. An employee of the ice company ran after them yelling for help. He got plenty. The game in progress at the time pitted the San Fernando Police Department against an office of the California Highway Patrol. Thirty officers took up the chase in their own cars and the suspects were quickly apprehended.[3]

Two clandestine lovers in London were discovered when the man slipped a disc while engaged in a midnight tryst in a tiny sports car. The woman, trapped under her pain-wracked 200-pound lover, managed to summon help by honking the horn with her foot. When firemen had to cut away the car frame in order to rescue the couple, the distraught woman sobbed, "How am I going to explain to my husband what has happened to his car?"[4]

Each of the above victims suffered from incredibly bad luck. Conditions beyond their control interfered with their plans and changed their lives. There was no way that they could reasonably predict the events that would be their undoing. They lost not because of some psychological need to fail, but because of forces over which they had no control. They were victims of chance, of bad luck. Or were they?

People have attributed their fortunes and misfortunes to luck and supernatural forces for thousands of years. As modern-day Westerners, however, we look with derision on those in Africa, Asia, or the Caribbean whose lives are governed by superstition and sorcery. We are amused to hear that Zambians believe eating eggs causes sterility, that coastal villagers of Ghana attribute supernatural characteristics to the whale, that political leaders in Haiti or Nigeria use voodoo or magical curses to defeat their enemies, or that Javanese peasants are convinced that pulling out a hair from the head of the ghost of a prostitute will make you rich. We consider such people to be uninformed and unenlightened. Our intelligence and superior scientific knowledge tell us that there is no basis in fact for such superstitious beliefs.

We obviously would never be so gullible as to take such ideas seriously.

Yet those of us who scoff at the superstitions of others may step over cracks on the sidewalk, avoid walking under ladders, or knock on wood for good luck. Americans today spend approximately $130 million each year on amulets and good luck charms. A recent Gallup Poll indicated that nearly 32 million Americans take astrology seriously. A Chicago firm that deals in magical equipment has had a run on crystal balls that sell for as much as $23 apiece. Even the objective, scientific field of computer technology has been infiltrated by superstition and magic. A research manager for the military computer program at Dynamics Research Corporation stated, "I hired everyone building the computer by zodiac signs under which they were born."[5] It has been said that at California's Hughes Aircraft Company, any unmanned space probe is accompanied in the control room by more crossed fingers, arms, and legs than are at a contortionists' convention.

Perhaps because so many contests seem to be determined by luck — either good or bad — athletes have become notorious for using superstitious practices in attempting to influence it. The manager who wears his lucky cap at every game, the shortstop who always places his glove on the top step of the dugout between innings, or the quarterback who always puts his left sock on first go through magic rituals, almost believing that their behavior will influence the gods of luck to favor them. Even at the bastion of intellect and rationality, Yale University, a hockey player warned that you must never say the word *shutout* in the locker room. Someone had done it the year before, with Yale winning 4–0. Ten minutes after going back on the ice, their lead had evaporated.[6]

After coach John McKay's expansion football team, the Tampa Bay Buccaneers, had lost their first twenty-four gamcs, McKay considered showing up for the next game in the nude.

"Maybe it'll be lucky," he said. "Maybe it'll distract the opposing quarterback.

"I've worn 24 different outfits for the 24 games we've lost. I have slept on my right side the night before a game, the left, my stomach, back, sitting up and on the floor.

"I go to church. I study different passages. I sing this song . . . that song. I eat this and then that at the pregame meal.

"I have flat tried everything else." [7]

Controlling the Uncontrollable

We have already discussed the anxiety associated with the feeling of helplessness and the need for people to feel that they have some degree of control over their lives. A person who falls ill or loses a poker game or has a flat tire at a particularly inopportune time can feel pretty helpless and frustrated unless there is some plausible explanation for the mishap. If all else fails, or if the person is unwilling to accept personal liability for the predicament, it can be attributed to an accident or bad luck.

Max Gunther, who has made an extensive study of the subject, defines luck as "events that influence your life and are seemingly beyond your control." [8] Of all forms of life, humans alone have the desire, as well as the ability, to exert a measure of control over their lives and to influence their destinies. Other species either adapt to the world as they find it or they become extinct. If humans don't like their environment, they set out to change it. The sense of being helpless and at the mercy of someone or something that has the power of life or death over them is not well tolerated by most people. Yet none of us is in complete control of our lives. We are all subject to the unforeseeable, the unexpected, the unknown, the unfamiliar. No matter how much we fear it or abhor it, deny it or ignore it, our lives are all influenced by forces over which we have little or no control — forces that we call luck, chance, or fate.

Psychologically speaking, the difference between fear and anxiety is that in fear the source of threat is known, whereas in anxiety it is not. Anxiety, therefore, is more distressing. We feel endangered but do not know why. If we know what it is that threatens us, we can possibly do something to protect ourselves. If not, at least labeling the source of danger helps us to look at it more objectively. Many persons who are ill find some sense of relief when their disease is diagnosed, even if the condition is incurable. At least they know what to expect. By attributing our losses to bad luck, we change the cause from an unknown to a known. Labeling the reason for failing *luck* doesn't really give us any more control over the failure, but it satisfies our demand for rationality, our need to know why things happen as they do, our desire to avoid the anxiety of the unknown. If something has a name, it exists. It is a known.

Good Luck and Bad Luck

The function of science is to cast light on the unknown. In the absence of scientific knowledge, we are forced to rely on less exacting explanations for why things happen, such as hypotheses, speculation, magic, superstition, mythology, or folklore. Primitive tribes attribute illness, death, and other harmful events to the sorcerer, who specializes in harmful magic. If a warrior wants to defeat an enemy, he can enlist the aid of a sorcerer to perform various rituals or curses in his behalf. To protect himself, the potential victim may then seek out a witch doctor who specializes in good magic. The witch doctor is an expert in detecting and thwarting bad magic and in fabricating healthy, lucky, and protective charms and amulets.

Good magic to counter bad magic takes many forms. Even though we may deny we believe in superstition, we may still avoid black cats, knock on wood to avoid bad luck, and throw spilled salt over our left shoulders. We carry rabbits' feet and hang horseshoes over our doorways. Airline pilots, perpetuating an old belief that saliva is an offering of the spirit to the gods, spit on a wheel after their preflight inspection.

Compulsive rituals, designed to allay anxiety, are carry-overs from primitive magical rites aimed at enticing the gods to do the bidding of humans. They are a kind of good magic used to stave off threats of the unknown and to reduce the feelings of helplessness. A child of three may demand a drink of water, a trip to the bathroom, another drink of water, a kiss from Mommy or Daddy, a teddy bear, a favorite blanket, a night-light, and another trip to the bathroom in exactly the same order night after night to overcome the dread of going to sleep and being overwhelmed by the darkness and loss of conscious control. A ten-year-old boy may try to convince himself that if he bounces a basketball a hundred times without missing, his parents will decide not to get a divorce. Repetitious hand washing, the world's best-known compulsion, was Lady Macbeth's symbolic attempt to rid herself of guilt.

Compulsive and superstitious behavior can be thought of as ways in which people seek to curry favor with the unknown forces that they feel may control their lives for better or for worse. By performing certain rituals, they hope to gain help in winning some objective, or at least protect themselves from the vicissitudes of evil omens or bad luck.

A Lucky Excuse

Since we are all victims of bad luck at one time or another, we are inclined to lend a sympathetic ear to the misfortunes of others. It is only when the degree of bad luck seems excessive that we are likely to question whether or not the storyteller is in fact a reliable reporter. Short of that, bad luck can be a convenient scapegoat for almost any kind of losing experience.

Unlike Thomas Jefferson, who stated, "I am a great believer in luck, and the harder I work, the more I have of it," there are some people who feel unlucky if they do not achieve their goals without effort. Failure due to poor judgment or a slipshod performance can be attributed to bad luck. Inability to make a sale or pass an examination can be blamed on chance rather than lack of preparation.

Karen thought of herself as one of the world's unluckiest persons. Although she put off studying until the night before a test and therefore could not read all of the assigned material, she invariably picked the wrong chapters to study. If she decided to cut class, the teacher would pick that day to give a surprise quiz. When she struck out playing softball, it was because the sun suddenly came out from behind the clouds and blinded her. It only rained on days that she forgot her umbrella. Rather than risk staying home on Saturday night, she accepted a date with a boy she didn't particularly like. An hour later she got a call from "the cutest guy in the class," who asked her to attend the same function. As luck would have it, by the time Karen got around to applying for the summer job she wanted, the position had already been filled. Given the choice of going to a party or joining her parents to entertain a visiting uncle, she naturally chose the party — which turned out to be a dud. The next day Karen found out that her uncle not only was the manager of her favorite rock star, but that the entertainer had joined him and her parents for dinner.

In listening to the plight of "unlucky" people like Karen, one begins to wonder where luck, as such, leaves off and avoidance of responsibility for one's own behavior begins. In most of the incidents Karen related, it would have been more accurate perhaps to say, "I screwed up." But for people who are unable to admit their own mistakes and shortcomings, it is handy to have a convenient excuse such as bad luck on which to blame their misfortunes.

Is Luck Due to Chance?

Students and observers of human behavior are aware that some people seem to be luckier than others. And there are all sorts of theories and explanations as to why some of us get more or less than our share of luck — be it good or bad. If it were randomly distributed, shouldn't we all have approximately the same?

Not necessarily, according to statisticians who have studied the subject.

Because the odds against being dealt a bridge hand containing thirteen spades or of black coming up twenty-five consecutive times on a roulette wheel are so large, when it does happen people are often at a loss to explain it in any terms other than luck. However, the proponents of probability theory maintain that if enough hands of cards are dealt and enough roulette wheels are spun, such things are bound to happen. If, for example, you deal out 635 billion hands of cards, you should get *one* that contains thirteen spades. It has to happen sometime to someone, but no one can predict when or to whom. And because of the rarity of its occurrence, few of us will be so favored.

If a thousand people buy raffle tickets on a new car at a charity bazaar, only one person is going to win. The other 999 will be losers. The chances are that many of those who lose will say something like, "I bought another raffle ticket and lost again. I am always unlucky. I never win." If they realized the odds against their winning, however, they would understand that they would have to participate in a thousand such drawings without winning before they could legitimately talk about bad luck. Even then, luck is a questionable excuse since the larger the sample, the more reliable are the odds. When the odds are a thousand to one against our winning, it is possible to buy two thousand raffle tickets and not win and then win three cars on the next thousand tickets. Or we could win five cars on the first ten tickets, and be considered extremely lucky, but not win again on the next 4990 drawings and feel that luck has deserted us.

Sometimes the odds against winning are not this obvious and it is even more difficult to see that we lose, not because of bad luck, but because of bad odds. Many times people lose money by investing in get-rich-quick schemes where the odds are stacked in favor of the promoter rather than the investor. Or they take unnecessary chances with their health and become sick or injured. Or they lose jobs because they underestimate the risk of continually being late for work or being inefficient in performing their duties. In such cases, people may attribute their plight to bad luck whereas in reality luck had little to do with their losing. It is more the result of inept gambling. Those who lose by bucking the odds might do well to contemplate *Runyon's Law* (devised by the late author and sportswriter Damon Runyon), "The race is not always to the swift, nor the battle to the strong, but that's the way to bet."

When Is Luck Not Luck?

Research studies have shown that people differ in their readiness to attribute success or failure to their own efforts or to forces outside themselves. This is known as *locus of control*. Those who, like Tennyson, believe that ". . . man is man and master of his fate" are said to have an internal locus of control, while those who do not feel in control of their destiny have an external locus of control.[9] Those with an external locus of control are more prone to believe in superstition, the supernatural, and luck than are those who have an internal locus of control.[10] Thus, personality differences play a role in how strongly we believe that luck governs our lives.

If we truly believe that we are masters of our fate, then we subscribe to the theory that we create our own luck. If things go badly for us, it is not because of the Will of Allah, or the bad magic of some sorcerer, or of fate, or predestination, or just plain bad luck. It is our own doing. When it is difficult to see a connection between cause and effect, those with an external locus of control are inclined to think there is no cause. Instead, they attribute the effect to luck or chance. Those with an internal locus of control may look for unconscious motivation — some may even blame themselves unnecessarily.

Thus far we have discussed fear of failure, fear of success, excessive guilt feelings, and other unconscious motives for losing. These unconscious, self-defeating needs may well manifest themselves in situations and behavior that might appear, on the surface, to be the result of bad luck. The underlying cause is often difficult to ferret out, however, and at times may be impossible to verify.

There is a story that the English novelist Charles Dickens

once became involved with an actress named Ellen Ternan and bought her an expensive bracelet. Leaving it to be engraved, he also left his own name and address with the jeweler. The bracelet was then delivered to Dickens' wife, Catherine. Who is to say that the mistake was due to the novelist's unconscious guilt or hostility or simply to his bad luck?

Suggestibility and Gullibility

When Ralph Waldo Emerson remarked that "Shallow men believe in luck," he was stating a commonly held viewpoint that those who are less knowledgeable are more likely to attribute the cause of unexplained events to luck than are the more sophisticated. Education, intelligence, and an inquisitive mind tend to lessen one's feelings of dependency upon unknown forces such as sorcery, superstition, luck, and fate. Primitive societies, to a greater degree than more advanced cultures, help foster a belief in the supernatural and take it much more seriously. It has frequently been so widely accepted and such an integral part of their culture that scientific development has been retarded.

Although intellectual enlightenment and skepticism make for doubting Thomases rather than believers, enlightenment can be a mixed blessing. Faith healing, placebos, and witchcraft work because people *believe* they will work. The human mind can exert a tremendous influence over the body when it is programmed to do so. Under hypnosis we can execute great feats of strength that we are otherwise unable to perform. In psychosomatic and hysterical illnesses, the mind plays a major role in affecting the body. Physicians and therapists are today experimenting with ways to teach people to use their minds to combat germs, infections, and even the spread of cancer. At the same time, when a sorcerer in parts of Africa sprinkles a trail of magic powder around a victim's hut, the belief in the sorcerer's power is so great that upon seeing the powder, victims have been known to die.

When ancient and modern beliefs clash, there is often a state of confusion and chaos in the wake. Such is true in some of the emerging nations where the educated and uneducated differ in their belief in the supernatural. Closer to home, the Hopi Indians used to believe that they would get pains in their legs if they stepped across the path of a snake. They would then seek out witch doctors, who were able to cure them. During the Second World War, however, white Army doctors convinced the Hopi that the witch doctors were not competent. The Hopis still got leg pains, but the witch doctors could no longer cure them. Neither could the Army doctors, since the Indians had no faith in them either.[11]

Much of what is attributed to luck may in reality be an outgrowth of limited understanding or of faulty beliefs. There is little difference between believing in luck and believing in superstition. To those who truly believe in either, the explanation is real, while to the skeptic such people are gullible — or worse. Whether gullible, suggestible, or ill informed, however, people who are convinced that they are losers because they were born under the wrong sign or are pursued by bad luck are difficult to dissuade. In addition, the negative attitudes and the feelings of helplessness stemming from such a belief may well perpetuate their bad luck.

Maybe I Should Have Stayed in Bed

If you have ever had a day when everything seemed to go wrong, or you have been on a losing streak that you couldn't explain logically, or you have been irritable and depressed for no apparent reason maybe it wasn't just a case of bad luck. Some people might say your biorhythms were down.

There is a wealth of scientific evidence that documents the effects of biological rhythms on sleep-wakefulness cycles, sex, mood, mental alertness, and many other aspects of human physiology and behavior. Such rhythms usually occur daily or monthly and tend to be similar in all persons, at least in those of the same sex. However, there has been growing interest during the past few years in a theory known as biorhythm, whose proponents claim that certain body cycles reflect the ebb and flow of life energy. This theory contends that each of us has a twenty-three-day physical cycle, a twenty-eight-day emotional cycle, and a thirty-three-day intellectual cycle that begins at the moment of our birth and influences our life from that time on. Supposedly we have good days when the cycles are up, poor days when they are down, and critical days when they pass from one to another. About once a year all three cycles are critical at the same time and we are then particularly vulnerable, especially to accidents.

Investigators who have charted the relationship between accidents and the biorhythms of the victims have come up with conflicting results. Scientists who have taken the theory seriously enough to put it to scientific scrutiny also disagree as to whether or not biorhythms have any impact on our behavior. In the meantime, a number of major companies have been charting the biorhythms of their employees in an attempt to reduce accidents. The management of the Dallas Cowboys keeps biorhythm charts on its players to help win football games, and Jackie Gleason consults his biorhythm chart before every important engagement.[12]

Although it seems probable that biorhythms will wind up

in the same class as astrology and numerology, as a fascinating pastime rather than a science, it is still another attempt to make the unpredictable predictable, the unknown known, and the uncontrolled controlled.

And Then There Is Bad Luck

Despite all of our attempts to make sense out of the forces that influence our lives and to give logical explanations to the things that happen to us that we don't understand, we are confronted with the perhaps unsettling conclusion that there is still such a thing as luck. It influences our lives in untold ways. How do you explain the fact that you happen to be in a certain restaurant, sitting in a particular chair, at the precise moment that a specific waitress trips and spills soup on your lap? Or that you plan an extravagant garden wedding for your daughter and for the first time in twenty years it rains on that particular day of the year? Or that the day you go fishing is the only day of the season the fish are not biting? Unless you believe in fate or predestination, you may be forced to admit that some failures are simply the result of bad luck.

Not all people believe in luck, however, and some seem determined to defy it — let us hope not all with the sad result that befell Richard Kirschman of San Francisco, who named his boat after the ill-fated passenger liners *Andrea Doria, Lusitania,* and *Titanic.* The *Andrea Lusitanic* sank on Memorial Day 1974.[13]

Chapter 9

The Bottom Line

Despite the preoccupation that most of us have with winning, we have found in our discussions so far that in many cases we are the primary cause of our losing. We verbally extol victory and abhor defeat, yet we frequently take steps to insure failure. This disparity between what we claim and what we do is the result of a gap between conscious and unconscious mental activity. Although we like to think of ourselves as rational beings, the fact remains that human behavior is less likely to be logical than psychological.

Logically we know that losing is an everyday occurrence and that even the most successful of us will experience a considerable amount of failure. Yet, despite its prevalence in every aspect of our lives, few of us deal with losing rationally. Even though there appears to be no logical reason for it, we often react to failure psychologically with a feeling of humiliation and a deep sense of loss in self-esteem. Intellectually, we know that becoming involved, striving to achieve, or interacting with other people all pose the risk of failing; but emotionally we too often feel that if we don't win 100 percent of the time, our own personal world will come to an end.

In attempting to understand the reasons behind the fan-

If we reduce all of life to its simplest dimensions, we are left with two factors, life and death. Characteristics essential for the perpetuation of life and of the species are programmed into every living thing. It is logical, then, to assume that there is something akin to what might be termed a survival instinct in human beings as well as in other species. If so, *a person's ultimate loss is his or her loss of life.*

Psychologists and other behavioral scientists generally agree that: (1) most behavior is purposeful; (2) except for reflex activity, behavior is learned; and (3) behavior is learned because in some way it is rewarding. Since an infant is unable to make very accurate discriminations, any threat, danger, or discomfort, whether physical or psychological, would appear to be regarded as a threat to life. The infant would mobilize whatever defenses are available for survival. Any behavior, rational or otherwise, that seems to reduce the threat will be learned. Other responses will not. At its most primitive level, the purpose of all behavior is to preserve life and stave off death.

When our lives are endangered, we experience the emotions of fear or anxiety, which act as warning signals and stimulate us to do something to eliminate the threat. If, in similar situations of danger, we have found that shouting or running or climbing a tree makes us feel safe and reduces our fear, we are likely to employ that behavior again. As long as it works, we are inclined to use it. In other words, because it is rewarding, we have learned a specific response to danger. In the process of living and learning, we gradually develop more and more sophisticated ways of coping with danger. However, just as the ultimate loss is the loss of life, *the first and most basic fear is the fear of dying.*

tastic and confusing psychological behavior of people, it
necessary to make sense out of nonsense, rationality out c
irrationality. This is not an easy task. The role of the psy
chologist who tries to do this is sometimes likened to that o
a detective who is called on to solve a difficult crime. In
both cases the sleuth must sort out the few legitimate clues
from a myriad of false leads and deliberate misrepre-
sentations in order to find out exactly what happened and
why. If the detective is successful in solving the crime and
the criminal confesses, everyone, except possibly the culprit,
is satisfied. On the other hand, the mystery involving an obsessive desire to be perfect, a phobiclike fear of losing, or an
unconscious need to fail is never as neatly solved.

The origins of such behavior are thought to lie in early
childhood. However, since infants are unable to describe the
causal events, psychologists are deprived of the triumph of
having their theories confirmed. The situation more nearly
parallels that of the criminal who is convicted as the result
of a brilliant and logical presentation of evidence but who is
led off to jail proclaiming his or her innocence. In the minds
of many, there will always be some question as to whether
or not the right verdict was reached.

The Fear of Death

Recognizing the limitations and the possible pitfalls in such
a venture, let us sort through the labyrinth of the human
mind and take a stab at solving the mystery of our irrational
attitudes toward winning and losing. We have already
looked at the role of the unconscious in the development of
guilt, a negative self-concept, fear of loss of control, masochism, and other aspects of losing behavior. But can we dig
deeper? Is there a common denominator, a bottom line?

Coping with the Fear of Death

Although there is considerable evidence for believing that the fear of dying is a universal phenomenon, there are many individuals who claim not to be afraid of death. Some of these people have simply repressed the fear so that they are no longer in touch with their feelings. A few, faced with the inevitability of death, have come to accept it gracefully. For most of us, however, the fear of dying plays more or less of a role in everything we do.

Sigmund Freud introduced the concept of ego defense mechanisms, those mental processes we each use to protect our psyches from various types of psychological onslaught.

As the ego, or the self, emerges in early childhood, it becomes the psychological counterpart of physical life. Because a young child is unable to make clear distinctions, no real difference is seen between danger to one's ego and danger to one's life. The threat is perceived as equally traumatic in either case. Consequently, the more endangered we feel in our formative years, the more defense mechanisms we will employ and the more tenaciously we will hang on to them as a means of self-protection. Our whole personality structure is, therefore, influenced to a large extent by the amount and kinds of defenses we develop in order to feel safe and secure.

It is probable that individuals with severe personality problems, such as neuroses and psychoses, perceive themselves as coming closer to dying in early childhood or infancy than did their more normal counterparts. Their perceptions may have been accurate or inaccurate. The threat may have been physiological or psychological. However, as a consequence of their perception these people have learned to be anxious, defensive, self-preoccupied, and overly concerned with what others think of them. They perceive the world around them as more threatening than rewarding, and they feel they must be on guard to protect themselves. Their fear of failure and rejection is the psychological equivalent of the fear of death. They are not necessarily conscious of a fear of dying, but they are unduly concerned about the fear of being destroyed psychologically, of losing the respect of others as well as their own tenuous self-respect.

Obviously, the person who truly enjoys life, who finds it exciting and fulfilling, stands to lose more by dying than does the one who is bored and unhappy. However, many neurotics try to lessen their intense fear of dying by making their lives so miserable and unrewarding that, by contrast, death actually looks inviting.

There are, of course, better ways of dealing with the problem, and each of us has our own solution. Children who are given an ample amount of security, love, and reassurance have less anxiety about death than those who are deprived and rejected, but no one is completely immune from the fear of death. Other things being equal, children whose parents provide them with adequate protection have an easier time coping with their anxieties and putting them in perspective.

Today there is considerable furor about the amount of violence children are exposed to in the comics and on television. How much violence a child can handle is a debatable question, but most children go through periods of playing war, cowboys and Indians, and similar games in order to work through their fears and anxieties about death. Being shot, "dying," then getting up to play again gradually desensitizes the child's fears. By role-playing, the child gets some feeling of knowing what death is all about and develops some degree of familiarity with it, making it somewhat less terrifying.

Many children use imagination to produce powerful

parent surrogates, ferocious animals, and other fantastic creatures with which to work out their fears. Since the child is the writer, producer, and director of the fantasy production, he or she can force the threatening figure to obey commands and to submit to the creator's orders, thus developing a sense of mastery over that which was once feared.

Dr. Selma Fraiberg, a child analyst, cites the case of Tony, who tried to solve his fears with a screwdriver. He became so adept at taking things apart to develop a sense of control over them that his house became a man-trap before he was old enough to talk.

> Like many other children around the age of two, Tony was afraid of the vacuum cleaner and its deafening roar. Some children overcome their fear by learning to control the switch, to put themselves in command of the noise. Others, with a preference for play-acting, may transform themselves into vacuum cleaners and prowl around the floor making ear-splitting noises. But Tony was not the play-acting type and it was not enough for him to know that the switch on the vacuum cleaner controlled the noise. He had to find the noise. A number of investigations were conducted over a period of time. Tiny screws and wheels were removed and lost in this frantic research; and finally this limping monster issued its dying croak and succumbed without giving up its secret.[1]

Short of intensive psychotherapy, it is not often easy to trace a specific fear or a particular attitude about losing to the original fear of death. The complex process of human learning and the unconscious utilization of defense mechanisms to avoid facing the truth compound the problem. Clinical experience, however, reveals that for those individuals for whom losing is the most traumatic, the game, the race, the election, the bet, or whatever, is not the sole cause of the emotional overreaction. The present loss triggers associative processes linking it to past losses and the anxiety and fears associated with them. The threatening experiences that happen very early in life are apt to be the most terrifying because as young children we are less capable of understanding and coping with them than we are later.

The child who is whisked away to the hospital for surgery, separated from home and parents, surrounded by strangers, and suffering from pain cannot help but experience a fear of death. Neither can a small child who feels abandoned by his or her parents for a prolonged period of time. Nor the infant whose hunger pangs go unheeded. The more intense the fear and the more helpless the child feels in overcoming it, the more likely it is that failure and losing will be viewed as overwhelming, traumatic experiences in the future. Even though the later failure presents a threat to the ego rather than to life itself, the subjective feelings of loss, abandonment, and desolation associated with earlier threats to life are reactivated. The more these emotions are exaggerated in relation to the reality of the present failure, the more irrational they appear.

PART II

What Happens to Losers

Between grief and nothing I will take grief.
— *William Faulkner*

Chapter 10

Down but Not Out

Whenever we lose something — whether it is a job, a friend, an important athletic contest, a sum of money, or anything else of value — we feel depressed. Depression is the emotional state associated with losing. It is nature's way of helping people endure deprivation and sorrow. Although depression is experienced as painful, like all human emotions and behaviors it is an essential part of an overall program of survival. If humans have anything approaching an instinct, it is a survival instinct. Our negative feelings like anger, fear, pain, and depression fit into that instinctual pattern as much as do pleasure, happiness, and love.

Even though depression is a natural reaction to loss, it can be excessive. If it gets out of hand, it can lead to extinction rather than survival. It is estimated that about 75 percent of depressed persons have suicidal thoughts, compared with only about 15 percent of the general population.

Everyone experiences depression from time to time in some degree. Depression is no respecter of age, race, religion, or socioeconomic status. It is found in infants, children, and adults. Among the rich and the poor. Among the famous and infamous. Abraham Lincoln became so depressed following the death of his first love, Ann Rutledge, that his friends feared he would commit suicide and took away his knives and razors. Winston Churchill was periodically beset with what he called his "black dog" of depression. Great writers such as Dostoevski and Edgar Allan Poe were victims of severe depression. Shakespeare captured the essence of depression in his characterization of Hamlet, who in a state of dejection exclaimed:

> "O God! God!
> How weary, stale, flat and unprofitable,
> Seem to me all the uses of this world!"

For most people who suffer depression following a loss, even a severe loss such as the death of a loved one, grief and mourning run their course in a reasonable length of time. Some people are more prone to depressive symptoms than others, however, and for them it takes longer and the severity is likely to be greater. Extreme depression involves neurotic and psychotic behavior and interferes with a person's ability to function in everyday activities.

Estimates of the incidence of depression vary since most individuals who have depressive symptoms never go for treatment and therefore never become a statistic. Also, in many cases depression is masked as headaches and other physical complaints, is dissolved in alcohol, or is treated chemically — with prescription drugs, over-the-counter mood elevators, or street drugs like heroin and cocaine. The National Institute of Mental Health recently estimated that eight million Americans are depressed to the point where they require professional help, that 125,000 are hospitalized each year for depression, and that perhaps another 200,000 should be. This is probably as accurate an estimate as any.

When You're Down, You're Down

The letdown feeling after losing a close ball game or the feeling of despair following the breakup of a love affair are easily recognized. Many times, however, depression is experienced by people who are unaware of what it is that they have lost, and sometimes by people who are not even aware that they are depressed. Part of the confusion is that the symptoms are so diffuse. Usually when we think of depression we conjure up a picture of someone who is sad, down in the dumps, unhappy. But that is only part of the depressive experience. Depression may affect every aspect of human life, particularly when it is severe.

Emotions

The unhappy mood, while perhaps the most obvious symptom of depression, is only one aspect of the syndrome. Terms used to describe the emotional state of the depressed person are numerous: sad, unhappy, blue, despondent, discouraged, gloomy, morbid, downhearted, miserable, dejected, wretched, lonely, grief-stricken, mournful. These feelings reflect the low emotional state of individuals who have suffered personal tragedy or loss. It matters little whether or not these people are aware of what it is that they have lost, and the feeling may not always appear rational by objective criteria. Some people wake up in the morning feeling depressed although they went to bed happy. Some feel depressed when to an outsider things appear to be going well for them. In fact, depression is so irrational that it is possible to feel as despondent and upset about losing a neurotic symptom in the course of psychotherapy as it is about losing a job or smashing up a new car.

Psychobiological Functions

A second category of symptoms that accompany depression is the disturbance of basic functions such as sleeping, eating, and sexual activity. Depressed individuals often lose interest in their environment and reduce the number of activities in which they engage. They no longer find pleasure in eating, conversing with friends and family, hobbies, entertainment, or even lovemaking. The typical pattern is a slowing down of all bodily functions, which results in loss of appetite, loss of sexual drive, and increased periods of inactivity.

In some cases, particularly if anxiety is present in addition to depression, there is likely to be a speeding up rather than a slowing down of activity. Persons suffering from what is sometimes called *agitated depression* are likely to pace the floor restlessly, wring their hands, and continually moan about their unhappiness and their transgressions.

Rather than losing interest in food, some depressed individuals eat almost compulsively. They seem to feel that by eating they can fill up the emptiness they experience as a result of having lost something perceived as almost a part of themselves.

Cognitive Symptoms

Mental as well as biological processes usually slow down with depression. Thinking seems to take great effort. Words and ideas are limited and, if expressed at all, tend to be short and repetitive. Depressed persons manifest an extremely low opinion of themselves. Being preoccupied with their unworthiness, they lament their sins and failures. Shortcomings are often exaggerated to the point that the depressed person gives the impression of bragging. It is not enough to be a sinner, the person claims to be the greatest sinner that ever lived.

It is not uncommon for depressed persons to lose interest in everyone and everything except themselves. In so doing, however, they concentrate on their worst features. They resist reassurances of their worth by others and insist on magnifying their inadequacies and inferiorities. Suicidal thoughts and fantasies are frequent.

Somatic Symptoms

While it often goes undetected, depression is the underlying factor in a large number of physical and somatic complaints. In his classical study of depression, "Mourning and Melancholia," Freud observed that physical rather than psychic symptoms often dominate the clinical picture in depressed patients.[1] Symptoms vary and they may affect any organ or system of the body. Headaches, backaches, diarrhea, endocrine disorders, and cardiovascular problems are frequent. In a seven-year study of depressed patients at the Presbyterian Hospital of New York, Dr. Stanley Lesse found that 34 percent of the patients had their depressive disturbances masked by somatic symptoms.[2]

Negative Outlook

In depression, the outlook is often characterized by a sense of helplessness and hopelessness. A mood of despair is usually evident. Overwhelmed by negativism, depressed persons view the world pessimistically. The future is seen as bleak and unrewarding and is anticipated with dread. Consequently, there is little incentive to engage in tasks that might ultimately prove rewarding and thus help reverse the depressive cycle.

Changes in Social and Interpersonal Relations

The person who makes a drastic change in lifestyle, begins to experiment sexually after years of inhibition, or suddenly decides to terminate a marriage may be reacting to underlying depression. Significant changes in interpersonal and social relationships are often the first signs of what may later blossom into more conventional clinical symptoms of depression. The feeling of needing change often stems from an awareness that a marriage, a job, or old friendships have lost some of their former meaning and satisfaction.

Carl Olmstead, after spending twenty years establishing a successful dental practice, felt that life was slipping away from him and that he needed a change. He gave up his practice and bought a marina and boat rental business in a resort area. When that proved unsuccessful, he sold it at a loss and moved back to the city. He told his wife he wanted a divorce and began dating younger women. He broke his ties with his church, which had been a meaningful part of his life, and he stopped seeing old friends. None of these major changes restored what Carl felt he had lost. In fact, he added the loss of his practice, the loss of his family, the loss of social and religious bonds, and loss of money to his earlier loss of satisfaction. Depression gradually became more apparent until it was necessary for him to seek psychiatric help.

After depression sets in, changes in interpersonal relationships also take place. Very often the depressed individual tends to withdraw from other people, to become isolated socially. Being around others, particularly people who are enjoying themselves, makes the depressed person feel even more isolated and unhappy by comparison.

While people who are depressed may complain of loneliness and the lack of friendship, their behavior helps perpetuate the very conditions they claim to dislike. It is not much fun to be around people who are unhappy and morose. In a sense, depression is contagious. If someone in a family is morbid and gloomy, it is bound to affect other family members. They may become frustrated in their inability to cheer up the depressed person and may lose patience with the constant complaining and pessimism. Since we can make ourselves unhappy by thinking depressing thoughts and recalling unhappy events, we generally try to avoid situations and people who are likely to bring about these reactions. Depression feeds on depression. To avoid feeling depressed ourselves, we often go out of our way to ignore the depressed individual, which then intensifies the feelings of aloneness and abandonment such a person already experiences.

How Low Can You Go?

While depression may not be a factor in all cases of suicide, for many who take their own lives suicide is the final expression of the depressive syndrome; it becomes the ultimate manifestation of unhappiness and self-loathing. The suicidal act, in addition to terminating one's misery, can be viewed as an expression of contempt for oneself. We tend to destroy only things we no longer value.

In countries that are strongly influenced by the Roman Catholic or Mohammedan faith, both of which firmly condemn suicide, the incidence of blatant self-destruction is quite low. Extreme depression is handled in other ways. In many European countries where Catholicism is not a major influence — especially West Germany, Hungary, Czechoslovakia, Finland, Sweden, and Denmark — suicide is more readily tolerated and suicide rates are high. In the highly ritualized suicidal acts that were once a part of the Japanese national tradition, depression as such was given little prominence. However, in *harakiri* (self-disembowelment), which was performed by the nobility and samurai when their failure caused loss or defeat to their honor, their emperor, or their lord, and in *shuniju* (lovers' suicide) a state of depression is easily implied.

While suicide is often a dramatic act and calls attention at least temporarily to the plight of the victim, there is a far larger number of depressed persons whose self-destructive behavior is less obvious and takes place over a longer period of time. Many depressed individuals turn to drugs that make them feel good. If they feel enough better, they may well be on their way to becoming hooked. Excessive eating or smoking, compulsive gambling, unnecessary speeding, criminal behavior, and other manifestations of excessive risk-taking may also be indirect acts of self-destruction. Some individuals try to ease their depression through drinking, and many alcoholics have some awareness that their drinking patterns are a suicidal equivalent, a slow form of self-destruction. Instead of killing themselves all at once, they gradually destroy their bodies and their minds. In addition, many lose their friends and families, their livelihoods, and their self-respect.

The Birth of the Blues

While any significant loss will trigger a depressive mood, authorities are not all in agreement as to why the intensity of the reaction is greater in some people than in others. Some blame it on heredity. Others attribute it to biochemical differences in our brains. There is, however, a considerable amount of research that suggests people who react most strongly to loss as adults are those who have suffered serious losses in childhood. Those whose depression is the most severe have learned from past experience to be depressed in reaction to significant losses. They become hypersensitive to losing. Any real loss, or a memory of a former loss, or even an unconscious representation of loss may trigger a depressive reaction.

Dr. Aaron Beck of the Depression Research Unit at Philadelphia General Hospital found in comparing depressed with nondepressed patients "that three times as many who've lost a parent during childhood will topple when there's some kind of serious loss during adulthood." [3] Studies of infant monkeys separated from their mothers show that they manifest behavioral and physiological changes consistent with depression. [4] Researchers at the National Institute of Mental Health found that depressed adults perceived their childhoods to have had a greater amount of emotional deprivation than did a matched group of normal subjects. [5]

Part of growing up involves the loosening of family ties. Each of us needs a certain amount of love, understanding, and security in order to make an optimal transition from helpless dependency in infancy to relative independence in adulthood. If through the death or desertion of a parent, serious injury or illness, or emotional deprivation we lose our stability and security, we not only react with depression to the immediate loss, but we condition ourselves to anticipate other losses along the way. When subsequent losses do occur, we not only react to them, but they trigger memories of previous losses. Thus a chain reaction of depression sets in, part of which is attributed to the present, part to the past.

In addition to a sense of loss, guilt feelings are often an integral part of depression. Much of the self-condemnation and the self-destructive behavior associated with depression is a manifestation of guilt. It is not uncommon for depressed persons to blame themselves for the losses they incur. Children, in particular, often resort to a kind of magical think-

ing in which they erroneously connect cause with effect and
blame themselves for events over which they have no control.

When Annette was five years old her parents were divorced. After a stormy marriage of seven years and a
number of separations, Annette's mother finally filed for
divorce when her husband, in a drunken rage, attacked her
physically. Annette and her mother moved into a small
apartment and her mother went to work to support them.
Although she was unable to verbalize it, Annette felt that
she was responsible for her parents' divorce and for her
mother's subsequent unhappiness. She "reasoned" that if
she had been a better girl her parents would have been
happy and would not have separated. She vowed that she
would improve and they would then be a family again. Occasionally Annette would misbehave or become angry at one
or both parents. She would later blame these incidents for
the failure of her parents to reconcile. When her father re-
married, Annette became despondent, refused to eat for several days, and was extremely lethargic. Her mother was
shocked to hear Annette, who was then only eight, say she
wished she were dead.

In later years whenever Annette lost a tennis match, she
went out of her way to find fault with her game. When a
relationship with a man ended, she assumed total responsibility for the failure. Having lost a desired promotion to a
woman who was having an affair with their mutual boss,
Annette blamed herself for the loss by attributing it to the
fact that she had not worked harder.

Like most children who develop excessive degrees of guilt,
Annette was encouraged to do so. Before her parents' divorce, Annette's father would react to her misbehavior by
telling her how much it hurt him. When she visited him after
the divorce, he would remind her to be a "good girl" and to

look after her mother, implying that Annette was responsible not only for her own behavior but also for the emotional well-being of her parents. Annette was willing to assume the responsibility and guilt because that made her feel there was something she could do to change her unhappy plight instead of being helpless.

In addition to guilt and loss, a third factor common to depression is a tendency to internalize aggression, to turn it against oneself instead of against others. This originates as a self-protective device. In some families children learn that outward displays of aggression and anger will be punished. Any loss, however, is likely to precipitate angry feelings. If such feelings cannot be expressed openly, they must either be denied or turned inward. The Freudian theory of depression adds another dimension to internalized aggression. It stresses that the parent or parent substitute who withdraws love and security is hated by the child. Since the child cannot express that hatred against the adult for fear of retaliation, the child feels helpless and impotent. These feelings are resolved by identifying with the parent and internalizing the parent's hated characteristics. The child's hatred is then turned inward instead of outward, aimed at that part of the child's self that is like the parent, the child's original source of anger and frustration.

Aggression turned inward goes hand in hand with guilt. Depressed persons not only assume blame for every loss they experience, they are frustrated because the loss prevents them from achieving some goal. Since frustration leads to aggression and they have chosen to blame themselves for their frustration, aggression can logically only be turned against themselves. The resulting self-condemnation then intensifies the depression.

The Payoff

While depression, especially severe depression, is a most unpleasant experience, people are programmed to become depressed under certain conditions for very definite reasons. As with all negative experiences, we tend to avoid looking at and dealing with depression whenever we can. When depression occurs, our first impulse is to get rid of it as soon as possible. In some cases this is necessary or desirable. Yet, depression serves a purpose and is sometimes best endured rather than avoided.

The first and perhaps most important survival function of depression takes place in infancy. The infant who senses the loss of love and nurturance or feels abandoned by the mother or mother substitute will begin to withdraw and psychomotor processes will slow down. Helpless and dependent upon his or her environment for survival, the infant cannot forage for food when left alone. Therefore, the depressive syndrome is nature's way of helping the infant conserve energy and thus survive longer without nurturance. Something similar occurs in severely depressed adults. In extreme depression there is usually an increase in the presence of suicidal thoughts. At the same time, there is more apathy and less energy available to put the suicidal desire into action. (Interestingly, the danger of suicide increases when the person becomes less depressed and feels more energetic.)

Guilt plays a role in depression to the extent that it is likely that the unpleasantness of the depressive experience itself is interpreted as punishment. In time the punishment eradicates guilt, and the individual's slate is wiped clean.

Mourning, which is a normal depressive reaction following the death of a loved one, is a time for sorting out memories. Some we retain and they become a part of us; others we let slip away. While this re-evaluation of our relationship with the person who has died is a difficult and painful task, it enables us to preserve some of what has been lost and we are better able to let go of the dead person psychologically — to let that person truly "rest in peace." If we are unable or unwilling to accept the loss and to deal with it by going through a period of mourning, we leave ourselves open for all kinds of emotional trauma later on. Those who deny their grief, bottle up their feelings, and play the brave soldier deprive themselves of the opportunity to work through their deepest feelings. Their frustration, anger, unhappiness, and sense of loss remain unresolved and thus may surface later at inappropriate times or places, or may contribute to internal tensions and conflicts.

In general, depression may be viewed as an indication that we have lost something important to our well-being, which we should take corrective steps to restore. Just as the red light on the dashboard indicates that the car is running low on oil, depression indicates that we need to replenish our loss in self-esteem. Too often, however, we try to deny or get rid of depression rather than listen to what it is trying to tell us. It is true that sometimes the red light goes on because of a short in the wiring rather than a shortage of oil. If that is the case, it is safe to ignore the warning. On the other hand, to overlook the signal and drive a long distance without oil can be disastrous.

Secondary Payoffs

As children we may find that if we lose a favorite toy or do poorly on an examination or lose a baseball game, our parents and friends are quick to console us. They reassure us of their love and try to bolster our sagging self-esteem. They sense what we need to overcome our unhappiness and to keep our depression at a minimum.

Sometimes, when other methods fail, adults resort to the same tactics that were successful in childhood. When they feel emotionally deprived, they may, for example, use depression to extract love and concern from others. Either consciously or unconsciously they may use depression to manipulate those around them. By inferring that her husband is the cause of her unhappiness, a wife may attempt to make him feel guilty and cause him to buy her presents or be more attentive. A young man who is fearful of being rejected may become depressed and avoid social situations rather than risk being turned down for a date. Unable to assume responsibility, a businessman may go into a deep depression whenever a crisis occurs, thus forcing his partner to make all of the crucial decisions.

In situations like this, the depression may be real but is exaggerated or persists longer than normal because the "sufferer" is receiving some secondary benefit from it. As long as depression is more rewarding than painful, the individual is reluctant to give it up.

The Antidote

Since depression is a reaction to loss, an appropriate remedy is dependent not only upon what is lost but upon a realistic evaluation of the importance of the loss and what options are available to deal with it. The following are some of those options.

1. Most of the available advice for "getting out of the dumps" involves some sort of physical or social activity. Forcing ourselves to become involved with people and expending energy on athletics, physical labor, social work and the like can sometimes be helpful in overcoming the lethargy

and self-preoccupation associated with depression. Although such activity deals only with symptoms rather than causes, at times that is all that is required. Just as aspirin may relieve a headache while the body takes care of the underlying cause, concentrating on other people and things may relieve some depression.

2. To the extent that depression is the result of aggression turned inward, it can be alleviated by getting angry at something or someone other than oneself. A psychologist who works successfully with seriously depressed patients often provokes them into becoming angry with him when he fears their depression is becoming too self-destructive. In this way the therapist can assess patients' anger, help them channel it into constructive outlets, and teach them to express it in ways that are not destructive to themselves or others. Assertiveness training workshops or books such as *Creative Aggression,* by psychologists George Bach and Herb Goldberg, can often be helpful.[6]

3. Since guilt is usually involved in depression it is helpful to find alternatives to self-punishment in reducing guilt. Seeking forgiveness is a much more positive answer. Although learning to forgive oneself is usually very difficult, it is equally as important as seeking forgiveness from others.

4. In the case of mourning or grief, it is frequently better to relax and let your emotions run their course than to fight them. Acceptance of both the loss and the resultant depression often makes them less painful and makes it possible to recover more quickly than if mourning is aggravated by conflict, tension, and denial.

5. Learning to open up and trust others with your feelings is a positive antidote to depression. People who habitually keep their problems and their feelings to themselves ordinarily have more difficulty when they become depressed than do those who are freer in expressing themselves.

6. Seeking professional help when it is necessary to deal

with severe depression is also important. Recent studies show that the suicide rate in northern New England is the highest in the country. Mental health experts attribute it to the Yankee tendency to hide feelings and to "keep a stiff upper lip." "They [Yankees] feel that to get help for their depression or mental problems is not only wrong, but a symptom of weakness," according to Dr. Stephen Soreff, Director of Emergency Psychiatry at the Maine Medical Center in Portland. "The admission of needing help is against the Yankee mentality and people are dying because of it." [7]

7. By far the best safeguard against depression is an abundance of love. The first manifestation of depression in infants involves a perception of being abandoned and the feeling of helplessness and hopelessness that ensues. Embedded in this experience is also the feeling of a loss of love. The symptoms disappear rapidly if the mother or mother substitute cuddles the baby and offers reassurance, security, and affection. Regardless of age, a feeling of love and of being loved can replace the feelings of desolation, emptiness, and low self-esteem that stem from depression. Love also tends to diffuse anger. "In the final analysis," Freud once observed, "we must love in order not to fall ill." Psychologist Arnold Hutschnecker has stated, "Depression is self-hate and its cure is love." [8]

Chapter 11

Losers Who
Changed the World

Because it is easier to deal with things once they are identified, people have a penchant for names and labels. If we are able to identify a particular sound as a creaking shutter or an offensive aroma as the smell of burning toast, we are generally able to take appropriate action in regard to the information we receive from our senses. Not knowing, on the other hand, often causes us to feel anxious and unsure of what course of action to pursue. By putting labels on people and trying to fit them into categories, however, we tend to obscure their uniqueness while emphasizing their similarities. This applies to groupings such as winners and losers, successes and failures. Winners don't always win, losers don't always lose, and what is considered success by one person may be considered failure by another.

Christopher Columbus sought a new trade route to India but failed miserably, missing his target by thousands of miles. Yet, in doing so, he discovered a whole new world. Thomas Edison, universally acknowledged as a genius, averaged one new patent every two weeks of his adult life. However, almost all of his triumphs came before he was forty years of age, while the latter half of his career was marked by an increasing number of failures. James

Lawrence, an American naval officer during the War of
1812, spurred his men on with his now famous battle cry,
"Don't give up the ship!" Heeding his own advice, he went
down with the ship when it was sunk by the British. One of
baseball's all-time great hitters, Babe Herman of the Brook-
lyn Dodgers, was so inept in playing the outfield that spectators often wondered which team he was playing for. He was
accused of trying to catch the ball with his head instead of
his glove. And, as bad as his fielding was, his base running
was worse — not because he was slow, but because he
sometimes ran the wrong way on the bases or ran past his
own teammates.[1]

Were these men winners or losers? Attributes by which
winning and losing are judged usually include such things as
fame, money, physical prowess, and achievement. People
who have made the biggest impact on the world are usually
considered winners, and theirs are the names that fill history
books and become legends. Yet many of these heroes seemingly had feet of clay, were failures in their own time, or
their losses and defeats are forgotten as we pay homage to
their victories. The distinction between being labeled a winner or a loser is often arbitrary. Let's take a look at a few of
the losers who have changed the world.

Mozart

Wolfgang Amadeus Mozart was born in Salzburg, Austria,
in 1756. He began composing music when he was five and
soon established a reputation as a child prodigy. His adult
life was quite different, however, and was characterized by
frustration and failure. He was treated by his employer, the
Archbishop of Salzburg, like a menial servant and subjected
to considerable abuse. Moving to Vienna did not improve

his fortunes. There he also encountered numerous frustrations and disappointments. He made powerful enemies, especially the influential court composer Antonio Salieri, who did everything he could to impede Mozart's progress. Compelled to earn a living by teaching and performing, Mozart lived in abject poverty.

Mozart's personal finances never improved significantly. He often found it necessary to borrow money in order to survive. Impoverished, his spirit crushed, and his body racked with pain from illness, he nevertheless continued to compose works of music, which only later were recognized as masterpieces. He died in Vienna in 1791. "After a pitiful ceremony, attended only by a handful of friends, Mozart was buried in a paupers' section of St. Mark's Cathedral, with no tombstone or cross to identify the place."[2]

Poe

Edgar Allan Poe, although finding periodic success during his lifetime, spent much of it as a loser by most criteria. Born in Boston in 1809, the son of itinerant actors, he was raised by Mr. and Mrs. John Allan of Richmond. Although orphaned by the age of three, Poe was never legally adopted by the Allans. Having a preoccupation with his legal and psychological identity, Poe devoted much of his literary talent to the pursuit of answers to questions concerning love, death, and identity.

From an early age it was obvious that Poe was a troubled young man. His plight was not helped by marrying his sickly thirteen-year-old cousin, his poor financial judgment, or his taste for alcohol. After his wife died of tuberculosis in 1847, Poe's excessive drinking and financial poverty ruined his own health. His life became chaotic. Attacks of delirium, suicide attempts, and a series of romantic entanglements followed in quick succession. Several times he planned marriage or vowed temperance but was unable to follow through with either.

While traveling from Richmond to New York in 1849, Poe disappeared in Baltimore for five days. When found, he was semiconscious and never recovered.

"To make tragedy complete, Poe had gathered his writing together, story and verse; he had revised and reedited them, adding many improvements and correcting minor errors — and then he had left them in the care of his most bitter and relentless enemy — and died. Scarcely was Poe's body cold before Rufus W. Griswold, his literary executor, was out in the New York newspapers with what, under the guise of an obituary, amounted to a major defamation of the poet's character, to a subtle sneering at and depreciation of his work."[3] Despite the tragedy of Poe's personal life, Poe's literary genius has had a pronounced effect on the literature of the world. Few writers have achieved the popularity and acclaim that Poe has received since his death.

Van Gogh

Born in Holland in 1853, Vincent van Gogh was a misfit in a world that could not appreciate his brilliance until after his death. His attempts to support himself as a clerk, a teacher, and a lay minister all ended in failure. His romantic overtures were rejected by the several women with whom he fell in love. After he took up painting, Van Gogh was largely subsidized by his younger brother. Although his talent was recognized by some of the leading artists of the time, he had difficulty selling his paintings.

After a quarrel, he tried to attack fellow artist Paul Gauguin with a razor. Filled with deep remorse at his behavior, Van Gogh fled to his room, cut off his ear, and delivered it to a brothel he frequented. For the next year and a half he was in and out of mental hospitals battling insanity. In July of 1890, he managed to obtain a revolver and killed himself.

Today, Van Gogh's paintings hang in most of the prominent museums of the world, and he is considered one of the spiritual fathers of Expressionism, the movement that emphasized the idea of emotional spontaneity in painting.

Goodyear

Charles Goodyear was obsessed with rubber. It dominated his whole adult life to the detriment of his health, his family, and his finances. Born in New Haven, Connecticut, in 1800, Goodyear had no formal education. At the age of twenty-one, he went into partnership with his father in a hardware business that later failed. That was the first of many losses and disappointments. Failure and poverty characterized Goodyear's life and, on more than one occasion, he spent time in debtors' prison. Not infrequently, his family existed on the charity of neighbors. Six of his twelve children died in infancy. By the time he was forty, Goodyear was dyspeptic, gout-racked, his health broken — able to get around only with the aid of crutches.

Most of Goodyear's troubles stemmed from his fanatic determination to transform raw rubber into a useful material that would not melt in the summer nor freeze in the winter. To pursue his experiments, he sold his watch, furniture, and even the dishes off the table. Nothing deterred him from his goal. Even time spent in jail was used to try to discover the unique properties of rubber and how to mold it to his satisfaction.

Goodyear accidentally discovered the process of vulcanizing rubber when he dropped a piece of the material that had been treated with sulfur on a hot stove. In time he refined this crude process and opened the door to the development of a whole new industry. While he could well have amassed a fortune from his discoveries, Goodyear used incredibly bad judgment in his business dealings and died in poverty.

Nation

Clearly the most colorful and controversial of the nineteenth-century temperance reformers was Carry Nation. While others decried the evils of alcohol from pulpit and podium, Mrs. Nation took direct action. With a Bible in one hand and a hatchet in the other, she smashed saloons across the country. Her forceful, unorthodox approach to the problem subjected her to ridicule and contempt. It also brought her international fame and helped bring about national prohibition.

Born in Kentucky in 1846 of well-to-do parents who lost their fortune during the Civil War, Carry studied to become a schoolteacher. Her first husband was an alcoholic who died shortly after they were married and left her with a retarded child. In 1877 she married David Nation, a lawyer and minister. As she became involved in temperance activities, she developed a religious zeal. She became convinced that her crusade was divinely inspired and that even her name was predestined. She apparently suffered from hallucinations, which she interpreted as divine visions. Garbed in a black dress and bonnet, she set out to rid the world of alcohol, tobacco, and immodesty. The fervor of her endeavors, however, sometimes led to violence. On occasion she was arrested and sent to prison for disturbing the peace. Her husband, unable to go along with her intense campaign, divorced her in 1901 on grounds of desertion.

Brown

John Brown was born in Connecticut in 1800. As a youth he was deeply religious and for a while studied for the ministry, but quit to learn the tanner's trade. The first fifty-five years of his life were spent in obscurity. He married twice and fathered twenty children, of whom twelve survived. He moved his family frequently, tried and failed in a number of business ventures, and was constantly in debt.

In 1854 five of Brown's sons moved to Kansas and became embroiled in the conflict between pro- and antislavery forces. When his children appealed to Brown for help, he traveled through the East, soliciting money and arms for the antislavery movement. "Without the shedding of blood," he vowed, "there could be no remission of sin in Kansas." In 1856 he led a raid on a proslavery settlement in Pottawatomie, killing five men in cold blood. The following year he killed another man in Missouri and was considered a criminal, with a price placed on his head, by both Missouri and the U.S. Government.

Although an outlaw, Brown was something of a folk hero in parts of New England. He was able to gain sympathy for his antislavery activities and to raise money for an impending invasion of the South to free slaves. In 1859 Brown and a small band of followers attacked the United States arsenal at Harpers Ferry, Virginia, presumably to steal arms for the invasion. His irrational and ill-conceived plan led to disaster, and he and all of his men were either captured or killed.

Brown was tried and hanged for his offense, in spite of the attempt by a number of his sympathizers to prove he was insane.

Despite the military fiasco at Harpers Ferry, the incident brought Brown and his cause considerable national attention. He was strongly condemned by some and wildly acclaimed by others. "The view that Brown was a martyr reached its strongest intensity among blacks. To them he was a man of moral courage, a benchmark figure whose social resolve had not waited upon taking a poll or achieving a consensus. A symbol, he conferred worth upon his followers. Black Americans regarded Brown as a deeply religious being to whom slavery was the sin of sins."[4]

Marx

Marx was born in Prussia in 1818. Both of his parents were descendants of a long line of rabbis, but Karl's father, barred from the practice of law as a Jew, converted to Lutheranism. Karl rejected both Christianity and Judaism, becoming an atheist. It was he who coined the aphorism, "Religion . . . is the opium of the people."

Karl Marx spent most of his life in exile. When the Prussian government suppressed the newspaper he was editing in 1843, Marx moved to Paris. In 1845 he was expelled by France and went to Brussels, where he lived for three years before being expelled by the Belgian government for his radicalism. From there he went back to Cologne. Less than a year later the Prussian government exiled him and he returned to Paris, but he was again expelled a few months later. The rest of Marx's life was spent in exile in London, where he lived a stateless existence. Britain denied him citizenship and Prussia refused to renaturalize him.

Marx and his wife, Jenny, had seven children, of whom four died in infancy or early childhood. Of his three remaining daughters, two later committed suicide.

Excessive smoking, wine drinking, and the consumption of heavily spiced foods may have contributed to Marx's many illnesses, many of them probably psychosomatic in nature. He was plagued in his later years with coughing, headaches, carbuncles, pleurisy, lung abscesses, toothaches, and liver disorders. In the final twelve years of his life, Marx was so incapacitated that he could do no sustained intellectual work.

Despite his superior intelligence and his extensive education, Marx lived out his exile in England in near poverty. His only income was as a contributor to the New York *Tribune,* at five dollars an article, and subsidies from his well-to-do friend and collaborator, Friedrich Engels.

The influence of Marx's theories was not great during his lifetime. After his death, with the growth of the labor movement, it increased enormously. As developed and applied by Lenin, Marxist theory became the backbone of Russian communism, and for millions of people in the Soviet Union and in other countries, Karl Marx is regarded as one of the outstanding men in world history. Millions of others disagree vehemently with his theories, but no one can deny his impact on the world.

Christ

The influence of Jesus Christ on the world needs no elaboration. By most criteria he could not be considered a great success in his lifetime, and by some he might be considered a loser. Certainly, he lost his life at an early age after having been betrayed by a friend. A story by an anonymous writer, which has been printed in countless newspapers and recited at Christmastime over many radio stations, illustrates the point.

Here is a young man who was born in an obscure village, the child of a peasant woman. He grew up in another village. He worked in a carpenter shop until he was 30, and then for three years he was an itinerant preacher.

He never wrote a book. He never held an office. He never owned a home. He never had a family. He never went to college.

He never put his foot inside a big city. He never traveled 200 miles from the place where he was born. He never did one of the things that usually accompany greatness. He had no credentials but himself.

While he was still a young man, the tide of public opinion turned against him. He was turned over to his enemies.

He went through the mockery of a trial. He was nailed to a cross between two thieves. While he was dying, his executioners gambled for the only piece of property he had on earth, and that was his coat.

When he was dead, he was laid in a borrowed grave through the pity of a friend.

Nineteen centuries have come and gone, and today he is the central figure of the human race and the leader of the column of progress.

I am far within the mark when I say that all the armies that ever marched, and all the navies that were ever built, and all the parliaments that ever sat, and all the kings that ever reigned — put together — have not affected the life of man upon this earth as has that One Solitary Life.

Chapter 12

If You Lose, Lose Big

California Institute of Technology is not generally known for its athletes. In any ten-year period it has probably won more Nobel Prizes than football games. Back in the late 1960s, however, Caltech basketball teams built quite a reputation and received more than their usual amount of coverage in the local press. Over a seven-year period they failed to win a game, losing sixty-four in a row.

In 1973 Bethel High School of Ohio started a trend that was to bring them national attention in the world of sports. Their football team lost fourteen straight games, being outscored by a total of 723–0.

If there is a moral to these stories, it is this: *to get the most out of losing, lose big.* While big winners make news, so do big losers. The person who loses a dollar on the spin of the wheel in a Las Vegas casino attracts no attention. The person who loses a thousand does. The fact that a thousand dollars may mean less to the big spender from Iran than the dollar does to the salesman from Topeka makes little difference.

While most of us dislike to lose under any condition, some losses are easier to take than others; and, under certain circumstances, such as losing with dignity or losing against overwhelming odds, failure can earn a certain amount of respectability. Losing big, however, stands in a class by itself. And bigness is what sets it apart. We have been conditioned to think that bigger is better, and that also applies to losing. There is a certain amount of status in being a big loser just as there is in being a big winner. And many big losers were formerly big winners.

Charlie Steen is a good example. In 1952 he discovered the first uranium in the United States and the richest mine in North America near Moab, Utah. At one time he was worth approximately $60 million, but by the end of 1969 Steen was bankrupt, owing over $6 million to about 300 creditors. It is questionable whether his climb from rags to riches or his fall from riches to rags received the most notoriety, but there is no question that the ability to lose that much money in such a short time is going to attract considerable attention.

The Steens not only lost a lot of money, but, like most who achieve fame through losing, did so with a flair. Not long after Charlie's discovery of uranium, they had their own private fleet of airplanes, a $250,000 yacht, and a mansion worth $1.3 million. At one time Steen owned some thirty different companies, but lost them all. "Oh, did I ever make some stupid investments when I began to diversify," he said. "For example, I got into the aircraft business, but I was manufacturing piston planes for businessmen when jets came in. It was like getting into the buggy whip business when the Model T was introduced. I dropped $3.5 million on that one." [1]

In a sense, losing big is similar to winning. Recognition is given to the person who stands out from the crowd, the person who is different. In some competitive events, a booby prize is awarded for the person who finishes last. If they cannot do better in a positive sense, then many persons prefer to gain attention by being the worst. Children who consistently misbehave in school often do so because of the recognition they receive from such behavior. If they don't do well enough academically or otherwise to excel, they prefer to gain attention by their truancy or delinquency, rather than being ignored. Some severely depressed people tend to exaggerate their so-called sins, as if to gain a feeling of distinction, even superiority, by establishing themselves as the worst people who ever lived.

Driven to Destroy

Some people are so obsessed with the desire for recognition and fame that they will go to any lengths to achieve it. Feeling inadequate and inferior, Arnold Downey dreamed of ways of obtaining a large amount of money. Not that he wanted to do anything in particular with the money, but he felt it would make him important. Although he was intelligent, reasonably good-looking, and made a fairly substantial living as a draftsman, his self-concept was extremely poor and he went out of his way to discount any responsibility for the successes he had in life. He felt particularly inadequate with women, and at the age of twenty-nine had had only a handful of dates in his life — all of them unsuccessful.

Because of the emptiness of his life and his feelings of depression, Arnold sought help through psychotherapy. The first few months of therapy were spent dealing with his preoccupation with notoriety and the elaborate schemes and fantasies by which he hoped to become notorious. The most desperate and bizarre of his get-fame-quick ideas was to highjack an airplane and hold it for ransom. In his fantasy, getting caught or even being killed was inconsequential. The thrill of being powerful, feared, and above all important were worth any price he had to pay.

The need for recognition, the desire to be "somebody" is not limited to the Arnold Downeys of the world. It is often a factor in the irrational behavior of people in all strata of society, and especially in delinquent crime. As one youth involved in a gang killing stated, "If I would of got the knife, I would have stabbed him. That would of gave me more of a buildup. People would have respected me for what I've done and things like that. They would say, 'There goes a cold killer.' "[2]

The archetype of the loser who seeks fame and glory through some outrageously destructive act is John Wilkes Booth. Even as a boy he was obsessed with becoming famous. At the age of fourteen, he told a friend that someday he would do something that would make his name famous and remembered for a thousand years after he had died. A few minutes before his assassination of Lincoln, the same thought was uppermost in Booth's mind. He remarked to a casual acquaintance, "When I leave the stage, I will be the most famous man in America."

Envious of the acclaim given to his father and older brothers for their acting ability, John tried unsuccessfully to compete with them. Although John was talented and showed great promise, his brother Edwin far surpassed him. While the rest of the Booth family were in sympathy with the North during the Civil War, John became an enthusiastic supporter of the Confederacy. Whether this was an outgrowth of his envy and an unconscious means of spiting his family is not known for sure. It has been suggested that his zeal and his delusional fear that Lincoln would become a "king" might explain why he half expected a hero's acclaim for his murderous act. In any event, at the age of twenty-seven, John Wilkes Booth fulfilled the destiny he had predicted thirteen years before and died "with the satisfaction of knowing I had done something no other man would probably ever do."[3]

In more recent times, the assassination of John F. Kennedy is somewhat similar to that of Abraham Lincoln. Lee Harvey Oswald, like Booth, was hungry for status and recognition. A loner and a rebel most of his life, Oswald was defiant of authority, in part because his father died before he was born and he lacked a significant authority figure with whom to identify. His resentment was readily apparent, as was his pathological need for a sense of superiority and recognition. Short of something sensational like the assassination of a president, Oswald might well have lived and died in relative anonymity.

Legendary Losers

Not all those who lose big do so for public recognition. They may or may not have some psychological need to fail, but their failure somehow captures the imagination of the public, which exaggerates their bravery or other positive attributes and builds them into legends.

George A. Custer, despite his involvement in a number of successful campaigns during the Civil War, would probably never have attracted much attention by historians or the general public had he not lost the Battle of the Little Bighorn. As it is, however, Custer and his "Last Stand" have been the subject of nearly a thousand paintings and illustrations and more than five hundred books and essays. Poets such as Ella Wheeler Wilcox and Henry Wadsworth Longfellow have immortalized him. A nationwide organization called the Little Bighorn Associates, complete with a newsletter, is devoted to the study of the Custer battle. Shrines

and monuments to Custer can be found at the battlefield in
Montana, at West Point, and in Monroe, Michigan.

People need heroes to emulate and causes to give their
lives meaning. Particularly in times of stress and despair, our
hopes are buoyed by examples of extreme gallantry and
courage. Our own misery or boredom is lessened by identifying with these exalted heroes, and we can participate
vicariously in their daring adventures. Thus, legends and
myths of heroic deeds exist and grow because they satisfy
the unconscious needs and desires of the people. The legendary outlaw Robin Hood, for example, has been a peren-
nial favorite of Americans as well as the British for generations. He is a symbol of freedom and rebellion against
oppressive authority, as well a manifestation of the archetype of getting something for nothing by stealing from the
rich and giving to the poor.

According to Professor Bruce Rubinstein of Pennsylvania
State University, the paradigm of the martyred warrior who
gains fame at least in part from losing a battle and his life is
as follows:

a) The hero and a small band are
b) Surrounded and overwhelmed by
c) A much larger force of
d) Racial or national aliens.
e) Rash courage or pride has led him to fight at all, and
f) Though the battle goes well at first,
g) Treason or cowardice among one or more of his men turns
   the tide.
h) A heroic stand is made in which
i) Many of the enemy are killed
j) On or near a mountain from which
k) Help has been summoned, though it is too late.
l) The hero spurns a chance to escape, preferring to die with
   his men.

m) Wielding a sword which has served him well in the past, the hero is

n) Among the last to die, if not the last.

o) One man, usually insignificant, survives and carries the news.

p) A eulogy is intoned over the hero's corpse, often by his slayer, but

q) The victors are punished by the vengeful comrades or countrymen of the hero.[4]

Not only does this formula fit General Custer, but it also applies generally to the eleventh-century French hero Roland, who was defeated by the Saracens; the English Sir Gawain in the Middle Ages; Saul of the Old Testament who, along with all of his men, was destroyed by the Philistines; the Spartan Leonidas; and many others, including Davy Crockett and the defenders of the Alamo.

Delusions of Invincibility

A small businessman who became a big businessman with the help of a few government contracts and a lot of luck developed the belief that he had the magic touch when it came to making money. "Everything I touch turns to gold!" he told his friends. He then turned his back on the products and business practices that had brought him success, ignored the counsel of trusted advisors, and lost everything he had worked twenty years to acquire in a high-risk venture that he knew little about.

While this particular businessman does not have a national reputation, his story is told repeatedly by a wide circle of friends and acquaintances. Whenever the name of Raymond Berger is mentioned by them, it is usually associated with his one big loss rather than his twenty years of smaller successes.

Essentially the same script could be used with a more renowned cast. General Robert E. Lee is most famous for his surrender to General Grant at Appomattox. He is also noted for his defeat at Gettysburg, which is generally considered the turning point for the North in the Civil War. In that battle, General Lee, considered one of the great strategists of the time and victor in a number of brilliant campaigns against great odds, made a colossal tactical error. Against the advice of his senior corps commander and against a Northern Army firmly entrenched with overwhelming advantages in manpower and artillery, Lee decided on a frontal attack — and lost badly.

Lee's irrational decision is hard to explain. Early in his career he had launched a similar attack on heavily gunned entrenchments of McClellan's army at Malvern Hill and had been defeated. And only a year before Lee had successfully defended such a position against a frontal attack by Union forces. Therefore, he had firsthand knowledge of the futility of attempting such an attack. One explanation for Lee's making this fatal decision is offered by Dr. Ezra Fox, who claims that "as early as the outbreak of the war, the feeling was generally prevalent throughout the Confederacy that one Southerner could lick any two Yankee tradesmen and mechanics." This attitude, coupled with a series of brilliant victories, "created in the Army of Northern Virginia a delusion, not merely that it was the superior of its oft-defeated opponent, the Army of the Potomac, which it again faced at Gettysburg, but that, under Lee's leadership it was actually invincible, in other words, militarily omnipotent." [5] This delusion, according to Fox, was undoubtedly shared by Lee himself.

The story of Robert E. Lee parallels to some degree that

of Napoleon. He, too, was a great military leader whose spectacular victories on the battlefield endeared him to his troops and spurred them to great heights. As with Lee, a succession of victories most likely created a feeling of invincibility, which in turn led to carelessness and poor judgment. Napoleon's pride, arrogance, and delusion of omnipotence led him occasionally to make unwise decisions and alienate friends, thus contributing to his spectacular downfall.

Although Napoleon was a military genius, a gifted ruler, and a dedicated reformer, the association that comes to the minds of many people when Napoleon's name is mentioned is Waterloo, a word now defined by Webster as "a decisive defeat." It has been said for generations that Napoleon sought to compensate for his short stature by becoming a powerful giant. But, like Goliath, giants are most often remembered for their downfalls.

Overconfidence, feelings of invincibility, and delusions of omnipotence may be thought of as differing degrees of the same psychological state that causes people to ignore reality and make unwise decisions. Believing themselves to be infallible, they act as if they did not have to adhere to either the laws of the land or of nature, and sooner or later they fall. It can happen to the fellow who has a winning streak at poker, the actress who stars in a succession of hits, a successful athlete, or the President of the United States.

Payola

Strangely enough, losing big sometimes pays off financially. One of the nation's favorite radio and television shows from the Second World War until the mid-1960s was "Queen for a Day." Contestants on the show competed with each other for the highest rating on an applause meter by seeing who could come up with the worst hard-luck story. Whoever had the saddest plight was proclaimed "Queen for a Day" and presented with appropriate prizes.

Some candidates for public office are so eager to get elected that they use their own money to help finance their campaigns. Losing an important election is always painful for a serious political candidate but the pain is compounded if one also spends a good deal of his or her own money in the losing effort. Most professional politicians protect themselves by not risking their own funds. They rely instead on friends, connections, fund-raisers, and contributions from their political party. The candidate who takes in more money than is spent can even make losing rewarding, financially anyway. Senator John Tunney, for example, had a $47,000 surplus from his 1976 campaign. As long as he paid income tax on it, the money was his. A county supervisor in California lost the primary election but came out $48,000 ahead. An editorial commenting on these lucky losers stated, "No one contributes to a politician or a political cause anticipating that the recipient will be able to buy a new car, a new house or take a trip to Rome with the donation. That's the way it is, however. No refunds." [6]

In recent times big losers, including most of the key figures in the Watergate scandal, have written best-selling books about their misadventures, thus capitalizing on their political demise. Prior to Watergate, the biggest scandal to rock Washington, D.C., for many years was the unfolding of the story of the wheelings and dealings of Bobby Baker, former majority secretary of the United States Senate and protégé of Lyndon Johnson. One of the most influential men in Washington, Baker used his power to amass a personal fortune. Although his loss of power did not produce any notable monetary rewards, except for the proceeds from the book he wrote since his release from prison, Baker, in many ways, gained more from his conviction on charges of larceny and income-tax evasion than he lost. In a verbal portrait of Bobby Baker, written after his conviction, Milton Viorst, longtime political reporter, had this to say:

> In Washington, where Earl Warren strolls home unnoticed up Connecticut Avenue, where Hubert Humphrey has trouble catching a taxi in the rain, where Dean Rusk gets ignored by the Statler's doorman, Bobby Baker still stops traffic.
>
> In the fanciest restaurant downtown, Bobby enters and is at once surrounded by proprietor, maitre d', headwaiter, chief busboy, sommelier and hatcheck girl, all inquiring after his well-being. As he weaves through the aisles to his table, he waves like a champ to admirers who smile and call out to him. When he is steated, waiters rush up to light his cigarette, bring him his favorite brand of Scotch, assure him that the specialty will be brought to him the way he likes it. As he dines, passersby greet him effusively. After he finishes, he leaves behind the warm glow that a generous tip from a beloved customer evokes. In Washington, obviously, Bobby Baker is somebody . . .
>
> In a city where politics is prosaic, piety is puzzling and power is perishable, Bobby Baker is more dazzling now than he ever was. He had everything that this city honored and he lost it. But in losing it, he showed to all of Washington what only the Senate had known: Bobby Baker has élan.[7]

Crime and Punishment

Criminals are rarely identified as such until they get caught. And the bigger the cookie jar, the more publicity and notoriety go to the person whose hand was found in it. The crook who pulls off a big heist or the manipulator who wheels and deals on a large scale is apt to receive more sympathy and acceptance — and to capture the imagination of far more people — than is the thug who knocks off the corner drugstore for a few dollars. Bobby Baker, for example, claimed that his fan mail was forty to one on the positive side.

Jesse James and Butch Cassidy have become folk heroes. So have Bonnie and Clyde. But who remembers the name of the three-time loser who was caught shoplifting at Woolworth's or the kid who was apprehended after stealing a purse from the old lady down the block? The cost of crime in the United States is approximately $100 billion a year. Therefore, the criminal whose take is only a few hundred dollars makes hardly a dent in the total take and, as such, is hardly newsworthy; a Robert Vesco or the head of a mafia family, though, is.

There is something about a lot of money that taps the fantasies of most people. It is not uncommon for most of us to say, and believe while saying it, "If I only had a million dollars, all my problems would be solved." It rarely occurs to us that this is an illusion rather than a reality. Consequently, when we read of some business executive who absconded with several million dollars and fled to Brazil, or of some sharp operator who obtained loans on the same used car from six different banks, or even of the queen of welfare fraud who obtained welfare checks from five different offices for forty imaginary children, we may well express a certain amount of admiration and envy. We may identify with their cleverness in pulling off such scams — even though they eventually get caught. And we may vicariously enjoy all of the good things we think the money might do for us.

It helps, of course, if the money is taken from some large, wealthy, impersonal entity like a big business or the government. We might feel too guilty in even fantasizing about stealing from ordinary people like ourselves, who would suffer personally from the loss. In contrast, since we are more likely to identify and empathize with the victim of a lesser crime, such as the owner of the neighborhood liquor store that gets robbed or the person whose car is stolen, our anger rather than our admiration is likely to be vented on the criminal.

It has long been held that the rich and powerful fare better in the courtroom than do the poor and the weak. The punishment does not *always* fit the crime. While minor criminals go to jail for extended periods of time, "Meyer Lansky, described by officials as 'chairman of the board of organized crime' in the U.S., is estimated to have put together a 300-million-dollar empire from the rackets, with dealings in gambling, narcotics, loan sharking and real estate. Yet Mr. Lansky has spent only three months and 16 days behind bars, and is free today." [8]

Although it would be untrue to state categorically that the bigger the crime, the less the punishment, inequities in justice have been observed in all times. About 600 B.C., Anacharsis stated, "Laws are like cobwebs, for any trifling or powerless thing fall into them, they hold it fast; but if a thing of any size falls into them, it breaks the mesh and escapes." Cornelius Vanderbilt put it more crudely when he snorted, "What do I care about the law? Hain't I got the power?" And, more recently, the humorist Art Buchwald commented, "Any company executive who overcharges the government more than $5 million will be fined $50 or have to go to traffic school three nights a week."

A year or so before his downfall, Billie Sol Estes, the fast-talking, Texas-style wheeler-dealer, lay minister, and friend of powerful government officials who had built a fortune on shady dealings and influential connections, gave an interviewer the formula for his success. While the underlying message may not be clear, it has a nice ring to it. The Biblical-sounding parable also is evidence of the glibness that makes hustlers like Estes so fascinating and caused investors to jump to loan him millions of dollars on nonexistent storage tanks.

"You win by losing, hold on by letting go, increase by diminishing, and multiply by dividing," said Billie Sol Estes. "These are the principles that have brought me success." [9]

Faith in Lemons

"Ford Motor Co. last week admitted for all to know that its Edsel car was one of the most expensive mistakes a U.S. corporation has ever made. After costing Ford $250-million to bring to market, the Edsel lost an estimated $200-million more during the nearly 2½ years it was in production." [10] Such was the lead paragraph in an article appearing in *Business Week* on November 28, 1959.

After much fanfare and a nationwide contest searching for an appropriate name for its new entry into the automotive field, the Edsel soon became the laughingstock of the industry. Edsel jokes were the rage on the nightclub circuit, and the name Edsel became a common synonym for failure.

While the number one lemon in the history of the United States auto industry is gone from the production line, faithful owners no longer have need for tears. Today there is an Edsel Owners' Club, which has 1500 members scattered through all fifty states and six foreign countries. The club publishes a quarterly magazine and holds an annual convention. And, perhaps best of all, an Edsel today is not only a status symbol, but in top condition is worth approximately twice as much as it cost new.

Failure Pays in Hollywood

"Hollywood only recognizes big successes and big failures," according to actor Joe Don Baker. "The greatest thing for your career is a well publicized flop. You can work for five years on that. If you've got four or five failures in a row you've got a track record." [11]

Anyone who watches television with a critical eye knows that some of the worst shows become hits while many of the better ones bomb out. Success and failure are not judged as much by the quality of a show as by how many sets are turned on and tuned in to a particular channel at any given hour. In an industry that creates fantasies for a fickle public, traditional values and standards do not necessarily apply. Veteran columnist Jerry Buck summarizes the value of failing in the television business as follows:

> In Hollywood, possibly unlike any other business community, the road to success can be paved with flops. There is upward mobility in failure.
>
> Look no further than Richard Burton and Elizabeth Taylor. They went from one box office disaster to another. Yet, the more turkeys they were in the more they seemed in demand . . .
>
> I know a producer who hasn't had a hit show in more than a decade. But he's still in there pitching — and the networks are still buying . . .
>
> Actors go from bomb to bomb. Although acting is inherently an insecure profession they do have an advantage. An actor is almost never blamed for a flop. After all, he's only saying what the writer puts down on paper and if he doesn't deliver it's the director's fault.
>
> •   •   •
>
> Writers who write unfunny comedies and incoherent dramas make a good living. Directors who hardly know which end of the camera to point at the actors are in demand.
>
> I've often wondered how everybody gets away with it. Even the most talented person can have a failure, but some people make a career of it. [12]

Jack Keough is remembered in the broadcasting business not for his successful kiddie show, but for pulling radio's most famous boner. Thinking his microphone was off instead of on, he ended his show with, "There! That ought to hold the little bastards for awhile." Radio has given recognition to other big losers as well. In the 1960s a radio station in New York City, with the appropriate call letters WINS, gave air time to the "Bomb of the Month," the song voted least likely to succeed.

To offset the prestigious Academy Award Oscar winners, the *Harvard Lampoon* has for many years been presenting its annual Movie Worst Awards to the year's worst films and actors. Not to be outdone, Hollywood fashion designer Mr. Blackwell, in the interest of better grooming, offers his Annual Worst Dressed Women Awards. Among those he cited for having particularly poor taste in clothing was Princess Anne, whom he described as "a royal auto mechanic. She looked like hell in America. But then her whole family has made the list. They seem to try so hard!" [13]

Last Pays Off in Sports

Athletics immediately come to mind whenever we think of the overemphasis on winning. Leo Durocher claimed that "good guys finish last," and Knute Rockne supposedly didn't want "good losers" because "they get in the habit of losing." Fans do not want to pay admission to see their team lose. They quickly lose interest in a loser. If fans do go to a game when the home team is no longer in contention for a championship, they may do so only to boo. Regardless of why a team loses, the coach's job is in jeopardy. Even winning coaches and managers get fired if their teams do not win the Super Bowl or the World Series. Despite this winning-is-everything tradition, losers in athletic competition have received some attention.

As an alternative to the hoopla given to the traditional top ten teams published weekly by the top two newswire services during the frantic fall football season, a bright young man by the name of Steve Harvey has come up with the Bottom Ten. It is now a syndicated feature that gives recognition to the worst college and professional football teams in the country. A typical Bottom Ten evaluation is as follows:

> Poor Marty Domres. Cursed with an offensive line good for nothing but mental blocks, the Baltimore quarterback is trampled weekly.
>
> It's affecting his passing, too. Sunday, in the Colts' 17–6 loss to Denver, he gave up four interceptions, prompting reports that coach Joe Thomas would try to cure his wobbly passing by giving him a spiral notebook.
>
> The Colts took over the Bottom Ten lead from the Jets, who defeated the Giants, 26–20, in a sudden death (or, as Curt Gowdy calls it, sudden victory).[14]

Most newspapers support their local athletic teams — win or lose. Sportswriters may become critical of the coach or manager at times or offer advice on how the team might improve, but rarely does the press treat a losing effort as dramatically as did the Minneapolis *Tribune* recently. It held a contest in which readers guessed the day the Minnesota Twins would mathematically be eliminated from the American League West race. First prize offered by the newspaper was two box seats for the Twins' final game. Second prize was four box seats.

A few years ago the Hollywood Park racetrack inaugurated Losers' Week for horseplayers with losing rather than winning systems. The object was to pick the horse that finished last instead of first, and fans competed for prizes such as a year of free haircuts at a barber college, a gift certificate for a "Born to Lose" tattoo, and a repossessed Edsel.

In order to help equalize the talent among the various teams, the National Football League has a policy in which the team that finishes last one year has the first draft pick of graduating college stars the following year. Considerable publicity is given to the first draft choice, who is inevitably an All-American and frequently the Heisman Trophy winner. But what about the player chosen last in the draft? In 1976 Newport Beach, California, decided to equalize the publicity attending the football draft by honoring the *last* chosen player. Under the guidance of Paul Salata, himself a former college and professional football player, Irrelevant Week came into being in this beach community.

The guest of honor the first year, Kelvin Kirk from the University of Dayton, rose to the occasion and gave an inspired performance. He arrived for the festivities a day late, took the wrong plane home, later reported to the wrong pro training camp, and then washed out in just three days. So successful was Irrelevant Week that when it was repeated the following year, Congressman Robert Badham, who represents the area, immortalized the occasion and the guest of honor by inserting the following message in the *Congressional Record:*

> Mr. Speaker, it is with a sense of pride that I rise to pay tribute to Jim Kelleher, who has become in Newport Beach, California, a symbol of what is great in America.
>
> Kelleher is distinguished by the fact he was the 335th draft choice. The only reason he was not 336th is that they quit at 335. The important thing is that he probably would not play for an NFL team next year anyway, and besides, no one can remember who drafted him because they lost his draft card.
>
> So that my colleagues will understand the importance of Irrelevant Week, I should like to explain that when the surf is up,

the combers are rolling at the Wedge and the westerly breezes are filling sails, irrelevant pursuits such as study, high finance and office hours become irrelevant.

It becomes important relevantwise, then, for all of us to take our minds off the less serious problems of the day such as the tinderbox in Africa, the crisis in the Mideast, shortage of energy, abundance of deficits, glut of rhetoric and blizzard of paperwork to honor Jim Kelleher.

As that great philosopher once said, "it isn't whether you win or lose, it's whether or not you sit on the bench and have the right to play out your option." So it is with Jim Kelleher, who may never even have an option to play out.

The world is full of Jim Kellehers, who happily play out their options every week, unaware of the Chinese proverb which exhorts us all to fish or cut bait and warns that when the going gets tough, the tough say, "Forget it, man, it's not relevant."

But if worse comes to worst and push comes to shove, we must pause for a moment and reflect on the conditions under which we live in America, under the finest and most equitable system known to mankind.

Thus we can be thankful that we have the right to be drafted by the NFL, or not be drafted by the NFL, and what is even more important, not to play football at all or even understand it and therefore not have to listen to Howard Cosell. I am proud Newport Beach has chosen Jim Kelleher to bring into focus the irrelevancies of our day and amidst the troubles facing the world. May Jim Kelleher have a long and happy life whether or not he ever plays in the National Football League.[15]

Big Bungling in Government

Government, which is constantly being taken to task for its errors and its bungling, has since 1975 come under fire from Senator William Proxmire of Wisconsin for its wasteful ways. Every month Proxmire issues his Golden Fleece

Award for the biggest waste of the taxpayers' money. Awards have gone to the Department of Agriculture for spending $46,000 for a study to determine how long it takes to cook breakfast, to the Federal Aviation Administration for paying $57,800 to take body measurements of airline stewardess trainees, and to the National Endowment for the Humanities, which spent $2500 of the taxpayers' money to study people who are rude and frustrated on the tennis court.[16]

The rewards for losing big today confirm the observation made many years ago by Lewis Morris, a signer of the Declaration of Independence, who stated, "High failure overleaps the bounds of low success."

PART III

Losing as a Positive Experience

Failure is, in a sense, the highway to success, inasmuch as every discovery of what is false leads us to seek earnestly after what is true, and every fresh experience points out some form of error which we shall afterward carefully avoid.

— *John Keats*

Chapter 13

Ouch!

When nine-year-old Scott Deindorfer asked a number of famous Americans their favorite sayings, actress Mary Tyler Moore replied, "I guess my favorite quotation comes from my ballet teacher, who said to me: 'If it doesn't hurt, you're not doing it right.' I think you can apply this admonition to a great deal more than dance!" [1]

Every dancer and every athlete knows that muscles grow and harden only from exercise. Our minds, our knowledge and understanding, and consequently the quality of our lives follow the same growth pattern. Psychological growth is the result of learning experiences, but, like our muscles, our minds atrophy from inactivity, while vigorous exercise is often painful.

Since we have a natural tendency to avoid pain, it requires a sufficient amount of self-discipline, dedication, or motivation to overcome the resistance to exercising our muscles and our brains and to do the things necessary to grow to our potential. As the great German writer Goethe put it, "Everybody wants to be somebody; nobody wants to grow."

The kinds of growth experiences that are the most painful, and, consequently, the ones we are most inclined to shy away from, are those that result from failure and defeat. At first this does not seem to pose much of a problem. If you have ever watched a young child learn to walk, you know that failures far outnumber successes. But this does not deter many youngsters for long. They get up, take a tenuous step, fall down, get up, and try again. If they waited until they could do it right the first time, they might never learn to walk.

Before long, however, children are subjected to the process of becoming socialized. Their behavior is shaped by those responsible for their education and guidance. They are taught what is acceptable and what is unacceptable behavior. How well they learn these lessons determines whether children earn the label of success or failure. Successful children are praised, rewarded, and exhibited proudly, while failures are punished, ridiculed, scolded, and isolated.

Schools take over where parents and the neighborhood leave off. Teachers also indoctrinate children with what is considered acceptable and unacceptable behavior and judge them by how well they conform to the standards of success that are set by the school and the community.

Concealing Failure

Because failure is so intolerable to parents, teachers, and society as a whole, children soon learn strategies for denying, concealing, and distorting their failures and for extolling their victories. If they fail in school, they are likely to drop out. If not, they may become chronic worriers and develop psychosomatic complaints. They may learn to cheat, bluff, guess, and use crib notes. Some develop a certain amount of glibness and attempt to charm their teachers. While these and other devices may stave off the worst aspects of failure, what learning does take place is apt to be superficial and diluted.

When students leave the classroom they are thus prepared to meet the realities of the business and professional communities, where it is at least equally unwise to admit any kind of failure or error. Not only one's self-image, but one's livelihood is frequently on the line.

A visitor from outer space investigating almost any large company or profession might, on superficial observation, go away thinking no one there ever made a mistake. The annual stockholders' report invariably has a glowing summary of the company's successes, and even a drop in sales or profits is neatly rationalized so that it appears to have a positive and promising effect on the company's future. Nowhere is there mention of the president's boner in pushing a negative line of merchandise or failing to anticipate adverse economic conditions.

Professional journals are notorious for not printing articles about research endeavors that flop. Because the idea of failure is so threatening, there appears to be fear that the professional image may become tarnished if human errors show up in print. It might be refreshing to read about some brilliantly deduced hypothesis, conjured up by an eminent scientist, which was rigorously tested and proved to have absolutely no validity whatsoever. Even more important, it might save hundreds of other investigators much time and energy testing the same hypothesis as they come upon it independently.

In the fields of psychology and psychiatry, there are hundreds of books on success in psychotherapy. Students, patients, and beginning therapists who read only this material have a misconception about the odds of psychotherapy being successful. On the other hand, it is very difficult to find a therapist brave enough to share his or her failures with the public: to admit making a wrong interpretation, or misunderstanding the urgency of the patient's need, or of failing to make a proper evaluation of the patient's problems. Yet, the beginning therapist, who is sure to make errors, is unprepared to deal with them and feels unrealistically inept — believing everyone else has a perfect record of success.

Failures in Organization Development and Change, a book published in 1978 in the field of organizational development, will, let's hope, set an example for other professions. It deals with failure and is intended to provide a learning experience for people in the field, a chance to learn from the mistakes of others. One of the failures cited by authors Philip Mirvis and David Berg illustrates the extent to which people go to conceal their mistakes.

A consultant was called in to effect a change in the organizational structure of a company. The consultant recommended more management participation, but when he was questioned about the relevance of his theory to the particular company, he became defensive. He scolded the managers and accused them of misinterpreting the material, and he did not share with them the possible drawbacks of the system. He promised them it would increase employee motivation and result in improved satisfaction and production. However, in the first few months, countless hours were wasted in trivial group decisions while individual expertise was ignored in an attempt by managers to become more democratic.

Because the consultant had "sold" the managers on the new system, they as well as he became ego-involved with its success and ignored the ever-increasing evidence that the system was failing. They publicly claimed that progress was slow but steady, although privately some of the managers worried that the new plan was responsible for rising turnover and production delays. Rather than admit their mistakes, they even began concealing information from their superiors in order to protect themselves. It was even hypothesized that, with the passage of time, the consultant might very well look back at this fiasco and convince himself it was actually a success.

"This is not an isolated incident," Mirvis and Berg explain. "In universities, consulting firms, and organizations change agents repudiate their failures and propagate their successes. This leaves the public with an inflated, but distorted, perspective on organization development. It also deprives practitioners and their clients of the opportunity to benefit from their own and the mistakes of others." [2] This creates a vicious cycle in that the illusion of infallibility creates unreal expectations of future successes; and minor, but realistic, successes are judged as failures.

Losing as a Learning Experience

Years ago when an aspiring young writer interviewed IBM president Thomas J. Watson, he was given some sage but unusual advice by the industrialist.

> "It's not exactly my line," Watson said, "but would you like me to give you a formula for writing success? It's quite simple, really. Double your rate of failure.
>
> "You're making a common mistake. You're thinking of failure as the enemy of success. But it isn't at all. Failure is a teacher — a harsh one perhaps, but the best. You say you have a desk full of rejected manuscripts? That's great! Every one of those manuscripts was rejected for a reason. Have you pulled them to pieces looking for that reason?
>
> "You can be discouraged by failure — or you can learn from it. So go ahead and make mistakes. Make all you can. Because,

remember that's where you'll find success. On the far side of failure."[3]

The first step in profiting from failure is finding the courage and willingness to face it. Most of us have been conditioned to feel stupid when we make mistakes, to expect humiliation when our failures and errors come to light. These attitudes are hard to break. It is easier to deny our faults and pretend we never make mistakes, but, in the long run, this is itself a costly error since it limits our ability to grow. Arthur Gordon, the man to whom Thomas Watson gave the success formula, went on to become a well-known author and editor. Following his conversation with Watson, Gordon had a new perspective on failure. "Somewhere inside me a basic attitude had shifted. A project turned down, a lot of rejected manuscripts — why, these were nothing to be ashamed of. They were rungs in a ladder — that was all. A wise and tolerant man had given me an idea. A simple idea, but a powerful one; if you can learn to learn from failure, you'll go pretty much where you want to go."[4]

Attitudes toward winning and losing develop early in life. Those who feel it necessary to deny their failures and pretend to be perfect have most likely grown up in an environment in which they felt that love and acceptance were conditional upon being "good." To do anything "wrong" led to humiliation, rejection, or excessive punishment. Overly severe negative reactions to failure and mistakes do not lessen their occurrence as much as they cause the child to become more adept at concealing them. If anything, the damage to self-worth and the increase in resentment resulting from excessive punishment will most likely increase the incidence of failure and unacceptable behavior.

Rosemary and Carol lived next door to each other since they were babies. When they were young they played together constantly, but as they grew older their interests and their personalities were less similar and they generally went their separate ways. Part of their differences stemmed from Rosemary's evaluation of Carol as a poor loser. If the two of them got into any sort of trouble, Carol would always put the blame solely on Rosemary, even though the escapade might have been her own idea.

Carol was physically larger and more athletically inclined than Rosemary and usually won if they played Ping-Pong, tether ball, or raced their bicycles. Rosemary excelled at Monopoly and other games requiring mental alertness and strategy but was rarely able to induce Carol to play with her. When she did, Carol would find numerous excuses for losing or claim that "it's just a dumb game" and pressure Rosemary to go outside and engage in some more vigorous activity.

Carol was never a very good student in school. When she brought home a poor report card, her father would make a scene and threaten to cut off her allowance and restrict her television privileges. Usually, however, her mother was willing to accept Carol's view that the teacher was being unfair. Between report cards, Carol would "forget" to bring home failure notices and never admitted to her parents that she did not understand her homework assignments. When she failed on quizzes, she would destroy her papers quickly and indicate to her classmates that she had done well on them.

Observing her natural ability, Carol's high-school physical education teacher encouraged her to try out for the swimming team. When the coach pointed out flaws in her kicking style and tried to show her how to improve her backstroke, Carol felt humiliated and quit the team. Friendships were also short-lived since Carol not only blamed others for every problem that developed, but she never learned from her mistakes. If a friendship broke up because she failed to keep her commitments, she denied any shortcoming and therefore saw no reason to change her behavior.

She subsequently lost other friends for the same unrecognized faults.

Rosemary did not enjoy losing, either. Like Carol, she came from a family that prided itself on achievement and worked hard for success. However, her parents accepted the fact that mistakes and failures were inevitable and usually tried to help Rosemary learn from them. When she was very young and spilled her milk, her mother, even though irritated, tried hard to keep from becoming too upset or scolding her. Later, when she failed an algebra test, her mother went over the problems with her and helped her to understand where she had gone wrong. Instead of punishing Rosemary when she squandered her allowance, her father tried to explain how she might better have spent it. Rather than "ground" her the first time Rosemary stayed out later on a date than she had promised, her parents told her their reasons for imposing limits. Even though their daughter had failed to adhere to their previous agreement, they explained that they expected her to do better the next time.

Rosemary's parents tried not to destroy her self-esteem nor stifle her spontaneity by over-reacting to her failures. They also made an effort to set a positive example by admitting their own mistakes. Rosemary was particularly impressed when her mother apologized for snapping at her unnecessarily when she was really irritated at something else, such as the washing machine breaking down unexpectedly. Their openness about revealing their own weaknesses and failings made it easier for Rosemary to do likewise, and it helped keep the lines of communication open. As long as her parents were comfortable in accepting their own limitations, Rosemary felt little need to hide her own, and, in sharing them with her parents, she was better able to learn from them.

There is an old saying that "failure can be a weight or it

can give you wings." Since we all fail sometimes, we can either choose to learn something from these experiences or not. We can let the loss drag us down and demoralize us or we can gain new knowledge and understanding from it.

From our own experience as children, and possibly also as parents or teachers, we know that there are two fundamental ways in which we learn. We learn *to do* some things because we are rewarded for doing them, and we learn *not to do* other things because we are punished for doing them. Psychologists who make a career of studying learning tell us that rewards are more effective in most learning situations than is punishment. Since we are rewarded only for our successes, this would seem to negate the role of failure as a learning agent. However, *the recognition of our mistakes and the ability to distinguish between right and wrong answers* is often an essential part of the learning experience.

In one typical learning experiment, a psychologist places a rat in a box that has a grilled metal floor. The grill is electrified so that it shocks the rat's paws. However, there is a pedal in the box, and, if the rat presses it, the shock will stop. When placed in the box the rat will run, jump, squeal, and bite at the grill. Sooner or later it will press the pedal and the shock will stop. After the tenth trial, the average rat will go directly to the pedal and press it.[5] The rat has now learned the correct response and is rewarded by having the shock stop. However, during the first nine trials, the rat suffered various degrees of failure and learned that running, jumping, squealing, and biting would not solve that particular problem. If it had not learned from its mistakes, the results would have been fatal.

In the parlor game Twenty Questions, no one expects to guess the correct answer the first time. By learning from our wrong guesses, however, we hope to narrow the number of possibilities and ultimately arrive at the correct answer.

Schoolteachers sometimes use devices like this to help children learn to think logically. For example, a teacher may use Twenty Questions to help track down a number between 1 and 10,000. But, as one very perceptive teacher observed, children who are traumatized by failure find this a very anxiety-producing experience.

> They still cling stubbornly to the idea that the only good answer is a *yes* answer. This, of course, is the result of their miseducation, in which "right answers" are the only ones that pay off. They have not learned how to learn from a mistake, or even that learning from mistakes is possible. If they say, "Is the number between 5,000 and 10,000?" and I say *yes,* they cheer; if I say *no,* they groan, even though they get exactly the same amount of information in either case. The more anxious ones will, over and over again, ask questions that have already been answered, just for the satisfaction of hearing a *yes.*[6]

Even Computers Learn from Mistakes

Those simulated brains known as computers have been programmed to play games such as ticktacktoe. In playing with mere humans, these machines never lose — ultimately, that is. Built into the programming is an auto-corrective process by which a mistake made once is never repeated. Only when all of the possible errors have been made and corrected is the computer infallible. If you have ever had a running argument with a computer over a utility bill, you know well that those machines do make mistakes — in spite of what some clerk tells you when you complain. Without an auto-corrective mechanism, a computer that receives wrong information once continues to make the same mistake over and over again. Take, for example, the experience of Skip Swenson of Reno, Nevada. He purchased a personalized license plate, which he thought had the perfect unpretentious title, NONE. However, he kept getting billed for parking tickets that were not his. Soon they amounted to $953. Finally, he got an explanation. "It seems, Swenson was told, that every time a Reno policeman gave a parking ticket to a car with no license plate and wrote the word *none,* the computer picked it up and charged Swenson for it." [7]

While it may seem that computer mistakes always penalize the consumer, there are exceptions. When Stan Mazanek was a senior at the University of Arizona, the Globe Life & Accident Insurance Company offered a once-only student discount life insurance policy. For $1 the company offered to sell a $5000 policy that was good for six months. For a lark, Mazanek insured his pet guppy, carefully and accurately filling out the application and listing the fish's height, weight, age and other vital statistics. When the guppy, which was named Fred Finn Mazanek, died, Stan notified Globe Life. Upon closer inspection of the policy, Globe representatives began to think something was fishy. They eventually struck a compromise with Fred's grief-stricken owner and settled the claim for $650. When asked to comment, Globe's owner John Singletary replied, "It's sort of funny, you'll have to admit. You know, we mass produce these policies and have about 340,000 of them in effect. He put a strange name on there for a fish, and our computer just isn't trained to catch fish, I guess." [8] You can bet, however, that Globe Life learned from its mistake. Neither Globe nor the computer will get caught again.

Growth through Failure

In addition to facilitating learning from our mistakes, failure, in proper dosages, can help us grow in other ways as well. If we had only known successes, our perspective of ourselves and the world would be distorted. We would exaggerate our strengths and underestimate the risks involved in future endeavors. Our overconfidence would most likely interfere with sound judgment and sooner or later we would be sure to fail. To a person having no previous experience with failure, however, losing could well become a shattering ordeal rather than an experience to be viewed philosophically.

Something akin to that happened to an All-American football player who had been on a winning team through his college career. After being drafted by the poorest team in the National Football League and having undergone a disastrous season in which his team lost every game, he was still bitter. "This has been very difficult for me," he said. "Winning has been part of my life. I will never adjust to losing. Losing has affected my personal life. Football shouldn't be that important, but to me it is . . . winning made life enjoyable. You wanted to go out, have a good time. Winning made you happy. Now, I not only do not want to go out, I don't even enjoy eating. And I can't sleep." [9] While no one likes to lose, few of us take it that hard.

If we take advantage of the opportunity, the experience of losing part of the time can help us put winning and losing in their proper perspectives. Losing can be a sobering experience, make us look at ourselves and our abilities realistically, and help us to mature. Another football player, the quarterback on a team that had lost three games after having been ranked number one in the country earlier in the season, was interviewed after bouncing back and winning decisively. "Losing is a growing experience," he said. "Because of last year, we fell into the trap of thinking we'd never lose again. But we found out that wasn't to be. Losing brought us down to earth, made us more determined and made us work harder." [10]

Another potential fallout from failure is the development of *compassion*. Although too many or too severe setbacks overwhelm us and make it difficult to cope, causing us to feel unhappy and bitter, the proper amount of defeat and suffering helps us to become empathic and understanding of others in similar circumstances. Losing is like learning a number of foreign languages: It helps you communicate with many more people. It is impossible to identify with the suffering of others if you have never been hurt, to know the agony of defeat if you have never lost, to feel compassion for others if you have never known distress. The desire to reach out to others and to offer help in time of need is one of the most noble of human qualities, but it is unlikely that many of us would ever develop such compassion had we not also at some time been on the bottom, needing a helping hand.

Losing, itself, has no virtue. What we do as a result of the defeat, however, is important. Losing can either destroy us or it can make us stronger. Although the choice is not always ours, without loss, stress, discomfort, unhappiness, and dissatisfaction to overcome, there is no opportunity for growth. If we are able to overcome most of these obstacles, life is richer and we grow in character and self-worth. Success and failure are not solely the result of competition with other people. Victory does not always go to the best person or the best team. The final test is, do we do our best, or do we fail ourselves?

Leaders of all persuasions are aware of the strength that comes from coping with hardship. Iron, which is heated cherry red, pounded with a sledgehammer, and immersed in cold water, emerges much stronger as a result of this ordeal. Human strength also is tempered through adversity. Ho Chi Minh, in typical Oriental style, observed, "The rice grain suffers under the blow of the pestle. But admire its whiteness once the ordeal is over. So it is with men and the world we live in. To be a man one must suffer the blows of misfortune." In typical Western phrasing, Theodore Roosevelt expressed a similar philosophy. "Life," he said, "belongs to the man who is actually in the arena — whose face is stained by the dust and sweat and blood. It belongs to those who try and fail, and rise to try again. Life is found by those who spend themselves for worthy causes; and even if they fail, they fail while daring greatly."

Chapter 14

The Myth of Perfection

"Look at me!" Kimberly said to her therapist. "No wonder no one cares about me. I'm ugly, and I'm dumb. I can't do anything right. If only I were perfect, then everyone would love me."

Her therapist, who had heard this same theme hundreds of times over the years, shook her head slowly and replied, "How could anyone *possibly* love you if you were perfect?"

Kimberly looked surprised. "What do you mean? I don't understand. Of course everyone would love me if I were perfect. Why wouldn't they?"

"They might respect you. Even be in awe of you. But certainly not love you. Those closest to you would probably even learn to hate you after a while."

"That's weird!"

"Not really, Kimberly. You told me you were in love with Joe. Would you say he's perfect?"

Kimberly thought for a moment, then laughed. "Well, hardly," she admitted. "Last night he kept me waiting for twenty minutes. Then he got lost on the way to the party. And when we were ready to leave, he couldn't find his keys."

"And do you love him any less because he was less than perfect?"

"No, but I would like it better if he weren't always late."

"I'm sure. But it is our imperfections which make us human. If we never made mistakes, we would be superhuman — some kind of God-like being who is beyond the reach of other people. How would you feel trying to relate to someone who was perfect? Suppose Joe were perfect, how would you feel knowing that every time you had an argument or a disagreement, he was always right? If he never made a mistake and you did, wouldn't it make you feel even more inadequate than you do now? You would always be comparing yourself unfavorably to him; always coming out on the short end.

"Your friends and family would seek only his advice and opinion, never yours. You would learn never to challenge his ideas, never venture an independent thought of your own. In time you would become more and more dependent upon him, and would risk losing your identity. As a result of all of this, your self-confidence and your self-esteem would dissipate, and it would be a miracle if you didn't begin to hate him for making you feel so inferior.

"While it is commendable to try to improve your faults and work toward the goal of perfection, just pray you never reach it. Perfection, rather than causing people to love you, would actually create a barrier between you and them, and thus add to your feelings of alienation."

Like Kimberly, a lot of people feel terrible when they make even a slight mistake, or don't know everything about everything, or have to ask for help or advice from someone else. They share a common fantasy that because they have been humiliated or ridiculed for their shortcomings in the past, they will be accepted and loved only if they have none in the present. Many even develop an elaborate pretense of infallibility. Let's take a look at what is involved in this widely held myth.

The Roots

A part of the responsibility of parents, schools, religious institutions, and society in general is to teach children how to function in the world. Since the infant has no conception of right or wrong, the difference between what is acceptable and unacceptable behavior must be learned. Ideally, also, a distinction is made between the act and the person who committed the act. The following statement has been said so often that it has lost its zing, but it is still true: in dealing with a child, it is important to communicate, "I love and approve of you as a person, but I do not approve and will not tolerate your stealing candy from the store (or hitting your little sister, or sassing me, or whatever)." People who grow up without having made this distinction overreact to any loss or error or imperfection because any shortcoming, real or imagined, is perceived as a threat to their worth as human beings.

In transforming children into acceptable members of society, a tremendous amount of learning must take place. However, where the offering of love is a reward for good behavior and the withholding of it becomes punishment for unacceptable behavior, the equation of love with perfectionism is easily established. Since children need to feel loved almost as much as they need to be fed, the withholding of love as a punishment is a terrifying threat to hang over their heads. It may force them to be good out of fear, not from a desire to please. And it will most likely cause them to conceal and deny their misbehavior.

To Err Is Human

Whether we like it or not, we live in an imperfect world. Most of us spend a good deal of time bemoaning the inefficiency of other people. "Nobody ever does anything right!" is a common complaint. If we have an expensive watch that needs repairing, it would be nice to know there is a watchmaker out there who would take such pride in his craft that he would not return the watch until it was perfect. No one would argue with the fact that life would be much easier and more enjoyable if everyone were conscientious and tried to do his or her best at all times. However, something short of perfection is probably the ideal.

The myth that being perfect will make one lovable was questioned by Kimberly's therapist. She pointed out that in a close relationship with someone who was perfect, one's own self-esteem would suffer immeasurably. She might also have mentioned that the illusion of perfection implies that one is totally self-sufficient and, therefore, needs nothing from other people. On the other hand, the basis of any close relationship, including a love relationship, is mutual need. We have a need to be needed. If you infer that you are perfect and thus you neither need nor want anything from other people, you effectively shut people out of your life. If there is nothing they can offer you or do for you, they cannot contribute to the relationship. They feel unwanted and unneeded, and therefore unable to love you. The great Russian novelist Leo Tolstoy, who himself strove for perfection most of his life, observed, "We do not love people so much for the good they have done us, as for the good we have done them."

While many people verbalize the fantasy "if I were perfect, I would be lovable," it is possible that unconsciously they are trying to perpetuate their position of alienation. People like Kimberly view love with great ambivalence. It is both the most desired, yet the most frightening experience they can imagine. To say "I love you!" is handing another person the power to humiliate or reject them. This is so terrifying to such people that they dare not risk it. Instead, by their good deeds, their offers of help, and their "concern" for others, they seek assurance of love and caring from other people. At the same time, they protect themselves from feeling rejected if the affection is withdrawn by saying, in effect, "I am really self-sufficient and don't need your love."

Perfectionism thus is a defense against becoming dependent upon someone else. While supposedly attracting people, it keeps them at a safe distance. To love incurs risk. Perfectionists never gamble since they might lose; if they should lose, it would destroy their illusion of perfection. Any error, mistake, loss, or flaw threatens to topple their house of cards and they are terrified of being exposed for what they are — emotionally hungry individuals wanting desperately to be loved but fully expecting to be abandoned.

Obsession with being perfect takes much of the fun out of living. Life becomes a very serious matter if we are constantly concerned with whether our hair is mussed, our clothes are impeccable and in the latest style, our speech is perfect and every word is pronounced correctly, our ideas above challenge, and every action, every movement we make is exactly right. It is difficult to relax under such conditions. Any new undertaking is viewed as a painful and humiliating experience until it is mastered completely. We would exclude ourselves from activities that others find enjoyable because we have not become experts in them. By setting impossible goals for ourselves, we would be frustrated and unhappy much of the time. There is no joy in getting a spare if you demand a strike, in shooting a birdie if you expect a hole-in-one, in writing a great novel if your goal is the Nobel Prize, or in doing your best at anything if it is less than perfect.

If you demand perfection from others as well as yourself, you also make life unpleasant for them. Encouragement to do well is healthy but to continually pressure others to exceed their human capabilities is demoralizing. Few tolerate it for long. The old Italian proverb "He that will have a perfect brother must resign himself to remain brotherless" says it very succinctly.

Perfectionists also have a tendency to feel superior to other people, which puts a further strain on personal relations. A person unable to identify with the failures and mistakes of others finds it difficult to be charitable or tolerant. Many perfectionists become arrogant and act as if other people were beneath them. Overwhelmed by their own sense of importance, they nonetheless lack one of the most important aspects of greatness — humility.

Regardless of how hard we strive for perfection, none of us ever achieves it, and perhaps we should be happy that we don't. We all lose, we all make mistakes, we all have our imperfections. To err is human. To come down out of the clouds and enter the human race, we must admit our faults as well as our assets, our weaknesses as well as our strengths.

But, in so doing, we put ourselves on a par with others and make it possible to relate — to love and hate, to win and lose, to fear and trust, to give and take. In essence, to live.

Chapter 15

Winning by Losing

A number of years ago, an Englishman by the name of Stephen Potter introduced to the world the concept of one-upmanship in a fascinating little book called *The Theory and Practice of Gamesmanship: Or the Art of Winning Games without Actually Cheating.*[1] The book presents various strategies for turning defeat into victory by psychologically demoralizing your opponent. Even though you may lose the actual game or match, by using certain ploys and gambits you can learn to win the interpersonal struggle with your opponent, thus robbing him or her of any *real feeling* of victory. For example, if you are competing against a superior chess player and you know little about the game, you might say after three or four moves, "Oh dear! I really goofed! I'm afraid I'll have to concede defeat." Then, placing your chess pieces back in the box, you wait for your opponent or someone in the audience to ask incredulously, "Why?" To which you reply, "Well, *obviously* because I moved my pawn to KB-four instead of KB-three, in twelve moves you would have me in checkmate!" Since it is *not* obvious to anyone else, you have now established yourself as the unquestioned chess expert.

Of much more importance than merely being a guide to

teach us how to get one-up on our friends and foes, *Games-manship* is a satire on our overemphasis on winning. If winning were not so important, the struggle to become one-up instead of one-down would have no meaning. Losing, itself, does not put a person in a one-down position; it is necessary to be defensive about the loss, to have one's ego at stake. While one-upmanship may have a humorous appeal, the best defense against a one-down feeling is not a better strategy for putting others down but to develop a more realistic perspective on losing. If we look at losing objectively, there are a number of ways we can either profit from losing or turn what looks like a failure into a success.

A Little Loss May Be a Victory

Since winning and losing are often relative, it is safe to say that a little loss beats a big one. In actual dollars the person who loses ten dollars at the racetrack is ahead of the one who loses a hundred. Even a small loss may be painful, but it is sometimes necessary to accept it gracefully in order to reverse a losing trend. The inability to admit a small mistake can frequently lead to making large mistakes or even cause us to overlook the opportunity of bailing out and devoting our energies to some other activity that would be rewarding.

Perhaps the biggest deterrent to admitting failure is a false sense of pride. When our egos become invested in our decisions, we put ourselves on the line. If the venture turns out to be successful, we feel intelligent, capable, even superior. If it fails, we see ourselves as stupid, inadequate, inferior. This can be devastating. Frequently, however, we have to ask ourselves how much we are able or willing to pay to protect our egos from the humiliation of losing.

Many people lose heavily in stock-market and other investments because they cannot admit their mistakes. If they are touted into a particular stock or pick it on the basis of faulty information, they cannot admit that they were duped or they made a mistake. They can't bring themselves to sell when a stock has only lost two points. Instead, they will watch it go down twenty points more while hoping desperately that time will vindicate their judgment and they will eventually make a killing on the stock. In the meantime, there may be other investments available to them that might make money, except that all of their capital is tied up in the losing venture.

Nearly everyone has been jilted some time or another. Millions of people identify with the feelings expressed in ever-popular blues songs. The heartache and pathos of the rejected lover have been the theme of hundreds of dramatic productions. Yet, as sad as it is to be left waiting at the church, it is far preferable to sharing an unhappy marriage that ends in a bitter divorce. The person who walks out on you and breaks your heart is really doing you a favor. Think how miserable you would be continuing a relationship with someone who cared that little about you.

It is natural to feel frustrated and angry and hurt and to go through a period of mourning when we are rejected by someone we love. But after the pain has subsided, it would be well to look at the relationship critically. Were you really that happy with the other person? Was that person really the right one for you? How much of the hurt was the result of injured pride? What would the future be like living with someone who didn't love you and only stayed around because he or she felt sorry for you or didn't have the courage to leave? In most cases, an objective evaluation would probably reveal that, despite the pain of losing, the ending of such a relationship was a blessing in disguise. Furthermore, if we could learn from the loss something about our own needs and why we picked this type of person in the first place, we may find a partner with whom we can have a much more rewarding relationship the next time around.

Those individuals whose egos are so fragile that they cannot admit the slightest mistake or defeat, regardless of the reality of their situation, are prone to turn small losses into big ones. For every hero who is unable to accept a minor defeat and plows ahead to overcome seemingly unsurmountable odds, there are hundreds of people who compound their losses under the same circumstances and turn a small defeat into a disaster.

Live to Fight Another Day

In our mad scramble to win at any cost, where winning is more important than "how you played the game," we are likely to overlook the wisdom penned by Oliver Goldsmith back in 1761:

> For he who fights and runs away
> May live to fight another day;
> But he who is in battle slain
> Can never rise and fight again.

Few losses are as disastrous as they seem at the moment of defeat. Caught up in the emotion of competition, winning may seem like the only important thing in the world. Everything else is secondary. The adrenalin flows; instincts and emotions take over. Reason subsides. And the idea of losing is unthinkable. The importance of the game itself is magnified in the minds of the contestants — whether the game is selling a customer an insurance policy, a World Series baseball game, or a sexual conquest. Many years ago, T.A.D. Jones, a Yale football coach, told his team before the annual game with their arch rival, "Gentlemen, you are about to play football for Yale against Harvard. Never in your lives will you do anything so important."

Such is the nature of competition. It brings out the best and the worst in people. Some rise to their highest potential; others sink to the depths, employing any devious means in order to win. It has been said that the only times winning is really important is in surgery and war. Yet, even in war, defeat is not necessarily the end of the line. Look what has happened to Japan and West Germany since being crushed in the Second World War. Forced to build new industrial plants with new and improved technology to replace those destroyed by the Allies, these two countries have become world powers in a very short time. Meanwhile, former industrial giants like Great Britain, and to a lesser extent the United States, slip farther behind because they can no longer compete successfully with their former enemies in certain key industries, such as steel production.

While few of us think of it at the time, to survive defeat is in itself an accomplishment, to survive with dignity is a victory. Veteran professional athletes have been known to break down and cry after losing a hard-fought game. But the mark of a true professional is the ability to bounce back after such a loss and not think of it as the end of the world. Dignity is not lost because people are temporarily overcome by emotion, but only if they find it necessary to make weak excuses for the defeat or are depressed or demoralized to an irrational degree. Occasionally we read of someone who commits suicide after having been rejected by a lover, or someone who jumps off a bridge because of a financial setback. Rather than backing away from the loss, analyzing the situation and themselves, and resting up before going back into the fray, they let defeat defeat them. They view life as a catastrophe and see no satisfactory way of coping with it.

Unfortunately, they view catastrophe from a Western rather than an Eastern point of view. Webster's defines *catastrophe* as "utter failure," whereas the ancient Chinese definition is "opportunity."

Despite his Oriental background, Donald Wang's ideas were predominantly Westernized. In high school, at the instigation of his best friend, he tried out for the gymnastic team. Almost from the beginning he knew it was a mistake. He was not particularly well coordinated and he lacked the sense of timing and rhythm necessary to develop a graceful routine on the bars or the rings. Having been indoctrinated with the idea of never giving up, however, Donald persisted. Although he was not very interested in the sport, he forced himself to lift weights to build up his muscles and he worked diligently to master a simple routine on the side horse.

The following year, despite pressure from his friend, his teammates, and the coach, Donald decided not to compete in gymnastics. Instead, he tried out for the marching band, which he thoroughly enjoyed. Before long, he was playing second clarinet. When quizzed by his friend as to why he quit the gym team, Donald grinned and replied, "During the summer I stayed up late one night watching an old W. C. Fields movie, and something he said really made sense to me."

"What was that?" his friend asked.

"If at first you don't succeed, try, try again. Then quit. There's no use being a damn fool about it."

Unlike Donald, many individuals allow themselves to become locked into unpleasant or difficult situations because they are afraid of looking like a failure in their own or others' eyes. The fear of being thought a quitter or a coward is a strong motive to keep people trapped in unrewarding jobs, relationships, and numerous other activities. Painful as it is, admitting that one has made a mistake, or has been unable to measure up to the job, or even has failed miserably is often the key to walking away from a self-defeating situation — thus emerging victorious. If plowing straight ahead would always get us to our destinations, there would be no need for a reverse gear in our automobiles.

Is There a Message in Failure?

Our failures, like many other aspects of our behavior, are often attempts to communicate with ourselves. If we are able to tune in to the message, we may be surprised at what our failures are trying to tell us.

Sexual failures are a good example. Traditionally, problems such as impotence, premature ejaculation, and frigidity were considered symptomatic of a person's deep-seated sexual conflicts and inhibitions. Today, they are more often viewed as manifestations of unconscious communication between the sexual partners. A man's inability to maintain an erection, for example, may indicate that there is some unspoken conflict going on between him and his wife. He may be picking up hostile signals from her, which makes him less than amorous and not easily aroused. He, in turn, is perhaps responding angrily by withholding his emotions and punishing her by being unable to satisfy her sexually. If the couple is able to pick up the proper cues from his periodic impotency and can resolve their grievances openly and honestly, the sexual failures will most likely disappear.

There are many reasons why people lose their jobs. One of them is that they are in the wrong job. Carmen Rosales took a position as a salesperson in a department store after graduating from high school. Shortly after Christmas, she was laid off because business was slow. She next went to work for an insurance company, then a bank. After being fired from these positions, Carmen was quite depressed. She had always considered herself to be a capable, intelligent person, but now her self-confidence was shattered. She saw herself as a failure, while most of her friends were advancing in their careers. Finally, on the advice of a friend, Carmen went to see a vocational counselor. After taking a series of tests and talking at length with the counselor, she was able to see that the jobs she had chosen were incompatible with her interests and abilities. Being able to look at her previous job failures as an indication that she was not using her potential, rather than as a sign of inadequacy, was meaningful to Carmen and helped her regain her self-confidence. With her new feelings of optimism and self-assurance, she took a course that prepared her to become a travel agent. Her bilingual background, her love of travel, and her enthusiasm for helping people enjoy life made this an ideal occupation for her. After working for a successful travel agency for three years, Carmen is still excited about the travel business and is thinking seriously of opening her own agency in the near future.

Richard Carlyle was a bright, aggressive salesman. By the age of thirty, he had skyrocketed to the position of national sales manager for a large company. Shortly afterward, a bad turn in the market caused his company some sudden reverses. As the pressure to produce mounted, Richard found that his inexperience prevented him from doing the job that was demanded of him. Realizing that he was in over his head, he went to management and suggested that he be permitted to find someone to come into the organization over him and offered to either work with the person or resign.

Knowing that Richard had potential, and appreciating his

candor in recognizing his limitations, top management went along with his suggestion. They were able to hire a top sales manager, who had taken early retirement from another company, on a two-year contract. Before the two years were up, with coaching from the older man, Richard had acquired the necessary know-how to move again into the top spot and to run the department successfully.

Rather than deny his failure to do the job he was hired to do or let it demoralize him, Richard correctly interpreted the failure as an indication of his inexperience. He was then able to do something constructive to change the situation from a negative one to a positive one. If we do not turn a deaf ear to our mistakes and our failures, they often tell us loud and clear what our problems are and how to correct them.

Losing as Practice

Few people start at the top. In almost every worthwhile endeavor, success is dependent upon practice. The artist, the surgeon, the boxer, the accountant, and the dancer who try to reach the top in their respective fields devote months and years to perfecting their skills. They may be born with talent and intelligence, but success comes from developing their abilities through practice. Someone once asked a paratroop instructor what was the most difficult thing about parachute jumping. After thinking for a moment, he replied, "I guess it's that you've got to get it right the first time!" In most activities, however, we are not only allowed to make mistakes, we are expected to. The essence of practice is to correct those mistakes.

When first learning to type, we are likely to hit more wrong keys than right ones. And it may seem like forever before we can type a whole page without making a single error. If we learn to do that at ten words per minute, increasing our speed to twenty words per minute will also increase the number of errors we make. If we are not satisfied with typing at such a slow speed, we must be prepared to make more mistakes. Even the best typists make them at times.

Our dislike of failure may motivate us to work hard in order to overcome our errors and thus make us better typists, or musicians, or Ping-Pong players. However, we had better learn some degree of tolerance for error en route or we may well have ulcers by the time we have mastered the activity. In addition, if we become too frustrated and angry at ourselves for making mistakes, the added tension will most likely interfere with learning and actually *increase* the number of errors we commit.

The learning of any particular skill takes place in stages, known technically as a learning curve. Frequently, learning at first occurs rather rapidly, then tapers off for a while, increases again, and so on. At one or another of these plateaus, we are likely to stop learning unless challenged to go ahead. If, for example, after a few weeks of practice, you have learned to play a fairly good game of Ping-Pong, your future success will largely depend on your competition. If you only play with those who are much less proficient than you are, your game is likely to deteriorate. It is human nature to ease up when playing an inferior opponent. On the other hand, you will have to play a lot harder to lose respectably to a superior opponent. Playing against someone better than you are will challenge you, make you more alert, and motivate you to do better. In the process, you will most likely improve your game. Of even more importance, you may find that the exhilaration of performing at your peak in a hard-fought game with a worthy opponent far outweighs whatever negative valence there is in losing the game.

Losing the Fear of Losing

There is little satisfaction in defeating a significantly weaker opponent. Only bullies and those individuals who are terrified of losing find it rewarding. If you own all the houses in a game of Monopoly, it takes no further skill to defeat the other players. It is anticlimactic from there on. The true excitement of competition is to battle down to the wire with an opponent you respect. If you win, you have the feeling of accomplishment; if you lose, you have the satisfaction of having participated in a challenging and demanding competition. The pleasure, the enjoyment, the satisfaction of competition is destroyed to the extent that winning is more important than the contest itself or that the fear of losing prevents one from playing the game. The joy, the excitement, and, in some cases, the pageantry involved in competitive activities can themselves be sufficient rewards for participating if we can put winning and losing in proper perspective.

A very successful businessman went to see his physician because of recurring headaches and insomnia. When the doctor asked him what he did for fun, he replied, "I play a deadly game of tennis!"

The physician looked at him quizzically. "I said, 'for fun!'"

The patient thought for a long time and finally replied rather lamely, "We used to play bridge, but my wife ruined it because she wouldn't take it seriously enough. She would start talking and make some dumb mistake . . . and it didn't even seem to bother her. She would just laugh and say, 'Oh dear! I goofed again, didn't I?' How can you play bridge with someone like that?"

"Look, Max," the doctor said. "You're a nervous wreck.

All tied up in knots. Tension headaches. Can't sleep. Maybe I should write you a prescription for a tranquilizer, but I'm not going to. Instead, I'm going to prescribe a round of golf twice a week."

"But I've never held a golf club in my hands!" Max complained.

"I know. That's why I prescribed it. Furthermore, I don't want you to keep score. Or take lessons. Hack up the course all you want to, but replace the divots. Enjoy the exercise and the scenery, and forget about winning or losing. See if you can learn to relax and have a good time. If not, I'm going to have to prescribe something more drastic."

Much to his surprise, Max began looking forward to Tuesday and Friday afternoons. He put on an old pair of slacks and a sport shirt and headed for the municipal golf course with a set of secondhand clubs. Sometimes he played alone, but more often with a twosome or threesome that was teeing off at about the same time. Although his game gradually improved, he never kept score and was never sure whether he was winning or losing or whether he was doing better or worse than the time before. He concentrated on his swing, but he was also appreciative of the smell of freshly mowed grass and the patterns of clouds overhead, and he paid close attention to the people he played with, finding that he considered them more as interesting companions with whom he was spending a pleasant afternoon than as deadly enemies that he had to defeat.

Max is still a competitor and always will be. But it doesn't bother him if he misses a putt or hooks a drive. He will try to drive farther than his companions, but if his ball lands in the rough instead of on the fairway, he is as likely to laugh as to curse. By accepting the fact that he will never be the world's greatest golfer and learning to enjoy friendly competition on the course and a leisurely glass of beer in the clubhouse after, Max has added a new dimension to his life. Following his doctor's advice, he has found that it isn't always necessary to be number one and that losing, at least on the golf course, does not have to be a humiliating experience. By admitting his inadequacies and accepting defeat when it comes, he not only is rewarded by the fun of the game but also by the measurable improvement in his health — a reduction in tension and more nights of satisfying sleep.

Losing Enhances Winning

Without contrast, a black-and-white photograph does not differentiate dark and light areas and the picture turns out to be gray and uninteresting. The same is true with life. Without variation, it becomes dull and boring. For many persons, sameness means security and safety. They may prefer the monotony of repetitious routine to the risk of the unknown, which to them is frightening. Even something positive, like success, can be boring, however, if it is constant. If we achieved every goal we set for ourselves, our lives would be as gray and uninteresting as a photograph with no contrast.

Human beings, by and large, spend more time and effort trying to get the things they don't have than they do appreciating the things they do have. The child who is allowed to have an ice-cream bar every time the Good Humor truck comes by learns to take the ice-cream bar for granted. Before long ice cream loses its thrill. But for the child who receives ice cream only occasionally, it is a treat. When King Midas was able to turn everything he touched to gold, gold no longer had the same meaning for him. The tennis player who wins the club championship on the fifth try will most likely consider it a bigger thrill than if he or she had won it for the fifth time in a row.

When Diane was in elementary school, she was always at the top of her class. In high school she was a straight-A student and the valedictorian of her graduating class. Everyone, including Diane, expected her to be the brightest student in her grade, and no one was surprised when she was. It was pretty much taken for granted. When she went to the state university on a scholarship, her friends and family expected great things of her. There was talk of Phi Beta Kappa and summa cum laude, but, at the end of the first quarter, Diane's grades were one C, two B's, and an A. She was most upset. She had never had B's and C's. She didn't know how to face her family, and she considered dropping out of school.

After the immediate shock wore off, Diane went to see a school counselor. In discussing her problem, Diane had to admit that the competition was much stiffer at the university level than what she had encountered in elementary and high school. She also saw that her study habits were not the best, and that she would have to work harder than she was accustomed to if she expected to get top grades. By the end of her junior year, when she received A's in all of her classes for the first time, Diane had a real feeling of accomplishment. She had worked hard and learned a lot, and the pride and happiness she felt were much greater than that she had known during her elementary- and high-school careers. The thrill of winning again was enhanced by having been pushed out of the winner's circle for a while.

And the Last Shall Be First

It is not often that a team with a tragic losing record becomes the terror of the league, but surprisingly enough it happens. When Tampa Bay, of the National Football League, had a record of 0–23, John McVay, coach of the New York Giants, commented, "Right now they're the most feared team in pro football. Nobody wants to become the first team to lose to them."[2]

Occasionally, losing pays off in unpredictable ways. A handful of alcoholics, narcotic addicts, and criminals have found religion or a mission in life after having suffered considerable personal defeat and have used their own experiences to reach and help others. Organizations such as Alcoholics Anonymous and Teen Challenge operate under the premise that those who have previously lost to alcohol or drugs and have come back from defeat can best help others win their battles against dependency on these substances.

Of course, becoming an alcoholic, or an addict, or a criminal is a drastic price to pay for the opportunity of understanding these disorders. No one would recommend it. But even tragedy can sometimes have a positive fallout. As humans we have the potential to learn from the mistakes and defeats of others as well as our own. Consequently, even if people do not profit from their own misfortunes, others might. If a school building is destroyed by an earthquake, we try to develop materials and construction standards that will make future buildings earthquake-proof. Heavy casualties during time of war have resulted in great breakthroughs in the fields of medicine and science that have subsequently saved countless lives. A few accidents caused by a malfunctioning part may lead to the recall of thousands of automobiles and perhaps save many lives. The example of Helen Keller's fight to overcome her multiple handicaps has been an inspiration for millions.

A tragedy with a happy ending on a more personal level is found in an old Scandinavian story. While a fisherman and his sons were at sea, their house caught on fire and burned to the ground. His wife was beside herself when her husband returned home. All of their possessions had been destroyed. Yet the fisherman took the loss calmly. "A few hours ago," he said, "a storm came up and we were lost at sea. Then we saw a yellow light that guided us to shore. The fire that destroyed our house was the light that saved our lives."

What Price Victory?

In most endeavors, victory and defeat are not necessarily opposites. Frequently, we have to lose something to gain something. The questions then become: How much does it cost? Are we willing to pay the price? To become a successful business executive, it may be necessary to give up a certain amount of leisure time, to work long hours, to put yourself under considerable physical and emotional pressure, to subordinate your own interests and desires to those of the company. To be a world-class pianist or tennis player requires total dedication from early childhood, with little time for ordinary childhood activities. An obsession with money is almost a prerequisite for being financially successful unless you are born to wealth. This too often means putting everything else, including rewarding personal relationships, second. These are choices we all have to make if we desire to be successful.

If it is necessary to become dishonest in order to win, is

what you have won worth more than what you have lost in terms of self-respect? What is the price of victory if you lose your integrity? When winning means fame, money, and glory but the price of winning is loss of honor, decency, pride, self-esteem, and integrity, the choice may or may not be difficult to make. In the long run, choosing to lose the game, or the promotion, or the money results in the most important of all payoffs: being able to live with and respect yourself.

Hope for success and fear of failure are perhaps the two biggest burdens shouldered by the average American. "The thrill of victory and the agony of defeat" has become the credo by which too many of us approach life. Winning should be satisfying and it should be fun, but it is only fun when the price is not too high. Losing is rarely enjoyable, but it doesn't have to be disastrous. The purpose of life is not to win or lose but to improve and grow. We can do that either by losing or winning. The ability to put winning and losing in their proper perspective is therefore essential if we are to get the most out of living.

In the final analysis, whether we win or lose is less important than that we strive to play the game of life to its fullest. To do that requires taking chances.

Notes Index

Notes

Chapter 1: Win Some, Lose Some, pages 3–12

1. "Even Cheerleaders Quit Winless Team," *Orange Coast* (Calif.) *Daily Pilot*, March 23, 1977, p. B-1.
2. Sidney Harris, "Winning Isn't Most Important," *Orange Coast* (Calif.) *Daily Pilot*, August 9, 1977, p. A-6.
3. Warren E. Leary, "Overemphasizing Athletics Blamed," *Orange Coast* (Calif.) *Daily Pilot*, October 24, 1977, p. C-2.
4. Scott Ostler, "The Horse Shrink," *Los Angeles Times*, August 20, 1977, part III, p. 1.
5. Albert Ellis, "Rational-Emotive Psychotherapy," in William S. Sahakian, ed., *Psychotherapy and Counseling*, 2nd ed. (Chicago: Rand McNally, 1976), pp. 272–285.

Chapter 2: Who's Number One?, pages 13–23

1. John Dollard et al., *Frustration and Aggression* (New Haven: Yale University Press, 1939).
2. W. B. Cannon, *Bodily Changes in Pain, Hunger, Fear, and Rage* (New York: Appleton-Century-Crofts, 1929).
3. Walter McQuade and Ann Aikman, *Stress* (New York: E. P. Dutton, 1974), p. 106.
4. "Player Has Tooth Removed — from Leg," *Los Angeles Times*, October 13, 1970, part III, p. 4.

5. C. S. Dweck, "The Role of Expectations and Attributions in the Alleviation of Learned Helplessness," *Journal of Personality and Social Psychology* 31:4 (1975):674–85.
6. Robert E. Ornstein, *The Psychology of Consciousness* (San Francisco: W. H. Freeman, 1972), p. 51.

Chapter 3: Losing Is in the Eye of the Beholder, pages 24–34

1. Matt. 16:26.
2. Arthur W. Combs and Donald Snygg, *Individual Behavior* (New York: Harper & Row, 1959).
3. "Gosh, Everybody Makes Mistakes," *Los Angeles Times,* April 9, 1970, part I, p. 12.
4. "Morning Briefing," *Los Angeles Times,* October 12, 1973, part III, p. 2.
5. "Hey! Why Don't You Knock First," *Orange Coast* (Calif.) *Daily Pilot,* August 22, 1975, p. A-8.
6. Sigmund Freud, "Humor," in James Strachey, ed., *Collected Papers,* vol. 5 (New York: Basic Books, 1959), p. 2220.
7. Leonard Feinberg, *The Satirist* (New York: Citadel Press, 1965), p. 63.

Chapter 4: Striking Out with the Bases Loaded, pages 35–49

1. *Newsweek,* July 26, 1976, p. 56.
2. Matina S. Horner, "The Motive to Avoid Success and Changing Aspirations of College Women," in J. M. Bardwick, ed., *Readings on the Psychology of Women* (New York: Harper & Row, 1972).
3. N. T. Feather and J. G. Simon, "Fear of Success and Causal Attribution for Outcome," *Journal of Personality* 41:4 (December 1973):525–42.

Chapter 5: Striking Out with the Bases Empty, pages 50–64

1. Tom Koch, "What Is a Born Loser?" *Mad,* April 1967, pp. 24–25.

2. Anton Chekov, "Kashtanka," Constance Garnett, trans., *Select Tales of Tchehov,* vol. 2 (New York: Barnes & Noble, 1961), pp. 165–84.

3. Richard C. Teevan and Robert I. Fischer, "Hostile Press and Internal versus External Standards of Success and Failure," *Psychological Reports* 34 (1974):855–58.

4. Richard C. Teevan and Paul E. McGhee, "Childhood Development of Fear of Failure Motivation," *Journal of Personality and Social Psychology* 21:3 (March 1972):348.

5. Eric Berne, *Beyond Games and Scripts* (New York: Grove Press, 1976), p. 208.

6. Ibid., p. 201.

7. William Furlong, "Recap on Al Capp," *Saturday Evening Post,* Winter 1971, p. 45.

Chapter 6: The Joy of Losing, pages 65–81

1. Sam Janus, Barbara Bess, and Carol Saltus, *A Sexual Profile of Men in Power* (Englewood Cliffs, N.J.: Prentice-Hall, 1977), p. 95.

2. Edmund Bergler, *Curable and Incurable Neurotics* (New York: Liveright, 1961).

3. Charles Hillinger, "There Is a Momma," *Los Angeles Times,* March 1, 1978, part II, p. 8.

4. Dan Greenburg, *How to Be a Jewish Mother* (Los Angeles: Price, Stern, Sloan, 1976), p. 15.

Chapter 7: Heads You Win, Tails I Lose, pages 82–91

1. E. Kim Smith, "Effect of the Double-Bind Communication on the Anxiety Level of Normals," *Journal of Abnormal Psychology* 85 (1976):356–63.

2. Steve Mitchell, "Red Tape Stalls Beauty's Hoe," *Orange Coast* (Calif.) *Daily Pilot,* June 3, 1977, p. A-1.

3. William E. Simon, *A Time for Truth* (New York: Reader's Digest Press/McGraw-Hill Book Co., 1978), p. 183.

4. Sig Altman, *The Comic Image of the Jew* (Cranbury, N.J.: Fairleigh Dickinson University Press, 1971), p. 107.

Chapter 8: When Lady Luck Frowns, pages 92–105

1. "Parachutist Pays Dearly for Free Fall," *Los Angeles Times,* July 8, 1973, part I, p. 10.
2. "Woods Trip Backfires," *Orange Coast* (Calif.) *Daily Pilot,* October 30, 1976, p. A-9.
3. Narda A. Trout, "Robbery Suspects Caught Off Base," *Los Angeles Times,* May 12, 1974, part I, p. 1.
4. "This Tryst Takes on a Real Painful Twist," *Los Angeles Times,* October 31, 1977, part I, p. 6.
5. "That New Black Magic," *Time,* September 27, 1968, p. 42.
6. "Newsline," *Psychology Today,* September 1976, p. 30.
7. "Morning Briefing," *Los Angeles Times,* November 24, 1977, part III, p. 2.
8. Max Gunther, *The Luck Factor* (New York: Macmillan Publishing, 1977), p. 11.
9. Julian B. Rotter, "Generalized Expectancies for Internal versus External Control of Reinforcement," *Psychological Monographs* 80:1 (1966).
10. Rick J. Scheidt, "Belief in Supernatural Phenomena and Locus of Control," *Psychological Reports* 32 (1973): 1159–62.
11. L. M. Boyd, *Orange Coast* (Calif.) *Daily Pilot,* July 15, 1977, p. A-11.
12. "Those Biorhythms and Blues," *Time,* February 27, 1978, p. 50.
13. Jennings Parrott, *Los Angeles Times,* May 29, 1974, part I, p. 3.

Chapter 9: The Bottom Line, pages 106–112

1. Selma H. Fraiberg, *The Magic Years* (New York: Charles Scribner's Sons, 1959), p. 24.

Chapter 10: Down but Not Out, pages 115–130

1. Sigmund Freud, "Mourning and Melancholia," in *Collected Papers* (London: Hogarth Press, 1924).
2. Stanley Lesse, "Hypochondriasis and Psychosomatic Disorders Masking Depression," in Stanley Lesse, ed., *Masked Depression* (New York: Jason Aronson, Inc., 1974), pp. 60–61.
3. "Coping with Depression," *Newsweek,* January 8, 1973, p. 54.
4. Martin Reite et al., "Depression in Infant Monkeys: Physiological Correlates," *Psychosomatic Medicine* 36 (1974): 363–67.
5. Allen Raskin et al., "Factor Analyses of Normal and Depressed Patients' Memories of Parental Behavior," *Psychological Reports* 29 (1971): 871–79.
6. George R. Bach and Herb Goldberg, *Creative Aggression: The Art of Assertive Living* (Garden City, N.Y.: Doubleday, 1974).
7. "Suicides Linked to Yankee Stubbornness," *Los Angeles Times,* March 23, 1978, part I, p. 18.
8. Arnold A. Hutschnecker, "If You're Depressed, Know Why," *Vogue,* January 15, 1972, p. 103.

Chapter 11: Losers Who Changed the World, pages 131–140

1. Leo Rosten, "A Handful of Heroes," *Look,* December 13, 1966, p. 24.
2. David Ewen, ed., *The World of Great Composers* (Englewood Cliffs, N.J.: Prentice-Hall, 1962), p. 105.
3. Hervey Allen, ed., *Tales of Edgar Allan Poe* (New York: Random House, 1944), p. viii.
4. Benjamin Quarles, ed., *Blacks on John Brown* (Urbana, Ill.: University of Illinois Press, 1972), p. xiii.

Chapter 12: If You Lose, Lose Big, pages 141–160

1. Charles Hillinger, "Uranium Miner Once Worth $60 Million, Now Flat Broke," *Los Angeles Times*, October 19, 1969, part C, pp. 1–2.
2. Lewis Yablonsky, "The New Criminal: A Report on the 'Hip' Killer," *Saturday Review*, February 2, 1963, p. 55.
3. Philip Weissman, "Why Booth Killed Lincoln: A Psychoanalytic Study of a Historical Tragedy," in Norman Kiell, ed., *Psychological Studies of Famous Americans* (New York: Twayne Publishers, 1964), p. 146.
4. Bruce A. Rosenberg, "Custer and the Epic of Defeat," *Journal of American Folklore* 88 (1975):169–70.
5. Ezra G. Benedict Fox, "Was General Lee a Victim of Group Psychology?" in Norman Kiell, ed., *Psychological Studies*, pp. 218–19.
6. "Sometimes Losing Is the Way to Win," *Orange Coast* (Calif.) *Daily Pilot*, August 10, 1978, p. A-6.
7. Milton Viorst, *Hustlers and Heroes* (New York: Simon and Schuster, 1971), pp. 119–20.
8. "Crime's Big Payoff," *U. S. News & World Report*, February 9, 1976, p. 51.
9. "Winning by Losing," *Newsweek*, April 16, 1962, p. 94.
10. "The Edsel Dies, and Ford Regroups Survivors," *Business Week*, November 28, 1959, p. 27.
11. Jerry Buck, "Cleaning Up on Flops," *Orange Coast* (Calif.) *Daily Pilot*, May 27, 1978, p. B-6.
12. Ibid.
13. "Blackwell's '75 Losers," *Los Angeles Times*, January 8, 1976, part IV, p. 12.
14. Steve Harvey, "There's Help Available for Wake Forest," *Los Angeles Times*, November 12, 1974, part III, p. 3.
15. John Hall, "So What?" *Los Angeles Times*, June 22, 1977, part III, p. 3.
16. William Proxmire, "Golden Fleece: Defending Sunlight on Research," *Washington Post*, July 4, 1977, p. A-19-2.

Chapter 13: Ouch!, pages 163–176

1. "Dear Scott," *Ladies' Home Journal,* February 1978, p. 66.
2. Philip H. Mirvis and David N. Berg, eds., *Failures in Organization Development and Change* (New York: John Wiley & Sons, 1977), p. 3.
3. Arthur Gordon, "On the Far Side of Failure," *Reader's Digest,* September 1961, pp. 22–24.
4. Ibid., p. 24.
5. W. Ross Ashby, *Design for a Brain* (London: Chapman & Hall Ltd., 1960), pp. 108–9.
6. John Holt, *Why Children Fail* (New York: Pitman, 1964), p. 34.
7. "None Too Much for Computer," *Los Angeles Times,* January 12, 1978, part 1, p. 20.
8. "Fred's Policy Was Fishy — but Firm Bit," *Los Angeles Times,* April 7, 1974, part I, p. 12.
9. Earl Gustkey, "Former Trojans Endure Anguish at Tampa Bay," *Los Angeles Times,* November 4, 1977, part III, p. 7.
10. "Losing Made Us More Determined — Hertel," *Orange Coast* (Calif.) *Daily Pilot,* p. B-1.

Chapter 15: Winning by Losing, pages 183–199

1. Stephen Potter, *The Theory and Practice of Gamesmanship: Or the Art of Winning Games without Actually Cheating* (New York: Henry Holt and Company, 1948).
2. "Morning Briefing," *Los Angeles Times,* November 20, 1977, part III, p. 2.

Index